Editor
Heather Douglas

Illustrator
Mark Mason

Cover Artist
Brenda DiAntonis

Editor in Chief
Ina Massler Levin, M.A.

Creative Director
Karen J. Goldfluss, M.S. Ed.

Art Coordinator
Renée Christine Yates

Imaging
Ariyanna Simien

Publisher

Mary D. Smith, M.S. Ed.

Grade **3**

TCR 2913

Paired Passages

Linking Fact to Fiction

CORRELATED TO **COMMON CORE** STANDARDS

- Learn to differentiate between nonfiction and fiction.
- Build reading comprehension and critical thinking.
- See how fiction and nonfiction can be connected.
- Synthesize information from two contrasting passages.

Teacher Created Resources

Author

Ruth Foster, M.Ed.

Teacher Created Resources, Inc.
6421 Industry Way
Westminster, CA 92683
www.teachercreated.com

ISBN: 978-1-4206-2913-2

©2009 Teacher Created Resources, Inc.
Reprinted, 2013
Made in U.S.A.

Table of Contents

Introduction

> *Ann's guide gets in cars and rides on trains. Who is Ann's guide? It is a horse!*
> * * * * *
> *Boys and girls, you need to learn some manners! Who am I?*
> *My name is Toby. I am a horse.*

If a student read either one of these statements out of context, it is likely that the student would have a difficult time knowing which statement was fiction and which one was nonfiction. In addition, the student would have no idea how the two statements could be tied together or used to support an argument or idea.

If, on the other hand, the student read these statements in context and understood how they fit into an entire passage, the student would be able to answer with confidence that, as strange as it may seem, miniature horses are being trained and used as guide animals for the visually impaired. The student would then be able to compare, contrast, or tie this fact to the passage about Toby, a fictional guide horse, who describes his own training while telling children how they should behave when they chance upon a working guide horse. (Both passages deal with miniature guide horses. One describes what they can be trained to do while the other describes how they are trained.)

Many state tests now contain assessment sections that contain paired passages. After reading two passages, students are expected to differentiate between fiction and nonfiction passages. They are expected to see how the two are connected and understand the underlying connection, as well as how they are dissimilar. They are asked to demonstrate their understanding of the passages by answering multiple choice questions as well as providing written responses.

This is a multileveled task that draws on many different aspects of the reading and writing process. *Paired Passages Linking Fact to Fiction, Grade 3* was written to provide practice with this type of exercise and assessment. It provides:

- ✣ exercises that build reading comprehension
- ✣ exercises that develop the skills needed to break down and analyze story elements
- ✣ exercises that provide practice in keeping sequence and details from two sources separate
- ✣ exercises that provide practice in proper letter formation, spacing, and spelling
- ✣ practice with multiple choice questions
- ✣ practice with written response questions on individual passage themes
- ✣ practice with written response questions that utilize information from two contrasting passages

In short, this book was written so that students will develop and practice the skills it takes to compare and contrast fiction and nonfiction passages. If asked, "Is it true that some horses ride in cars?," students will know how to find and use information from two separate passages to answer the question. They will also be able to record their reasoned response detailing the how and why in a written form.

Using this Book

The Passages

There are 25 units in *Paired Passages: Linking Fact to Fiction*. Each individual unit contains two high-interest passages. The first passage is nonfiction. The second is fiction. Each passage is written at grade level with appropriate vocabulary and sentence structure. The passages are tied together with a common theme. Unit subjects run the gamut from gorilla heroes to floating islands.

The units may be done sequentially, but they do not have to be. A teacher may choose to go out of order or pick specific units at different times because of class interest or individual students' needs.

Units may be done as a class or assigned as individual work.

The Multiple Choice Questions

A page of multiple choice questions follows the two passages. The first question focuses on the nonfiction passage. The second question focuses on the fiction passage. Answer choices for these questions come only from the passage the question stem is referring to.

The third multiple choice question asks what both passages have in common.

The fourth and fifth questions require the student to differentiate between the passages and understand what topic is covered in each one, as the answer choices are drawn from both passages. A few of these questions will require a student to combine the information from both passages to infer or extrapolate the answer.

Students can answer multiple choice questions on the page by filling in the circle of the correct answer. Students can also answer multiple choice questions by filling in the answer sheet located on page 7. Using this page provides practice responding in a standardized-test format.

Written Responses

A page requiring written responses makes up the final page of each unit. The first two written responses vary depending on the unit. They may require sequencing of events by filling in boxes, making lists, or drawing and labeling a picture. Each response deals with only one of the passages. These exercises are written to provide students with a foundation for sorting and organizing information. They provide an exercise in referring back to and keeping two different pieces of literary prose separate in the reader's mind.

The final two written responses require higher level responses. First, the student is asked to write out the main theme of each passage with complete sentences. Lastly, the student is asked to respond to a question that requires thinking about or using information from both passages to answer.

A teacher's expectations of what is a satisfactory response on these last questions may change over the year, or it may vary depending on the level of the student. For example, at the beginning of the year or with some students, a teacher may accept phonetic spelling and lack of punctuation. As specific topics are covered in class and students become more mature, a teacher may begin to check spelling, capitalization, ending punctuation, etc. For the final response, a teacher may require a complete paragraph or two in correct form. Enough variation allows that all students, even ones deficient in grade-level writing skills or those with advanced writing skills, can participate.

Meeting Standards

Each passage and question in *Paired Passages: Linking Fact to Fiction* meets one or more of the following Common Core State Standards © Copyright 2010. National Governors Association Center for Best Practices and Council of Chief State School Officers. All rights reserved. For more information about the Common Core State Standards, go to *http://www.corestandards.org/*.

Literature Standards	Passage Title	Pages
Key Ideas and Details		
Standard 1: RL.3.1. Ask and answer questions to demonstrate understanding of a text, referring explicitly to the text as the basis for the answers.	all passages	
Standard 2: RL.3.2. Recount stories, including fables, folktales, and myths from diverse cultures; determine the central message, lesson, or moral and explain how it is conveyed through key details in the text.	The Identical Flowers Silly Rudolph How Marshall Knew Vacation Journal 2022 Hot Water in the Snow Aesop's Fable of the Thirsty Crow Getting What Kate Wanted The Rich Man's Contest An American Folktale: The Great Blue Ox The Warrior with a Weak Spot	21–23 25–27 29–31 33–35 49–51 65–67 69–71 77–79 81–83 89–91
Standard 3: RL.3.3. Describe characters in a story (e.g., their traits, motivations, or feelings) and explain how their actions contribute to the sequence of events.	all passages	
Craft and Structure		
Standard 4: RL.3.4. Determine the meaning of words and phrases as they are used in a text, distinguishing literal from nonliteral language.	all passages	
Integration of Knowledge and Ideas		
Standard 7: RL.3.7. Explain how specific aspects of a text's illustrations contribute to what is conveyed by the words in a story (e.g., create mood, emphasize aspects of a character or setting).	all passages	
Range of Reading and Level of Text Complexity		
Standard 10: RL.3.10. By the end of the year, read and comprehend literature, including stories, dramas, and poetry, at the high end of the grades 2–3 text complexity band independently and proficiently.	all passages	

Meeting Standards (cont.)

Informational Text Standards	Passage Title	Pages
Key Ideas and Details		
Standard 1: RI.3.1. Ask and answer questions to demonstrate understanding of a text, referring explicitly to the text as the basis for the answers.	all passages	
Standard 2: RI.3.2. Determine the main idea of a text; recount the key details and explain how they support the main idea.	all passages	
Standard 3: RI.3.3. Describe the relationship between a series of historical events, scientific ideas or concepts, or steps in technical procedures in a text, using language that pertains to time, sequence, and cause/effect.	Danger! Do Not Band! Danger! What the Insects Proved Why Astronauts Have Puffy Faces The Beetles that Ride When Grandfather Yellowtail's Braids Could Snap To Hold or Not to Hold What Leaks Out Animals with Closed Nostrils The Elephant that Made a Word	16, 18–19 20, 22–23 32, 34–35 36, 38–39 48, 50–51 52, 54–55 56, 58–59 68, 70–71 104, 106–107
Craft and Structure		
Standard 4: RI.3.4. Determine the meaning of general academic and domain-specific words and phrases in a text relevant to a grade 3 topic or subject area.	all passages	
Integration of Knowledge and Ideas		
Standard 7: RI.3.7. Use information gained from illustrations (e.g., maps, photographs) and the words in a text to demonstrate understanding of the text (e.g., where, when, why, and how key events occur).	all passages	
Standard 8: RI.3.8. Describe the logical connection between particular sentences and paragraphs in a text (e.g., comparison, cause/effect, first/second/third in a sequence).	all passages	
Standard 9: RI.3.9. Compare and contrast the most important points and key details presented in two texts on the same topic.	To Hold or Not to Hold/What Jillie Is Afraid Of	52–55
Range of Reading and Level of Text Complexity		
Standard 10: RI.3.10. By the end of the year, read and comprehend informational texts, including history/social studies, science, and technical texts, at the high end of the grades 2–3 text complexity band independently and proficiently.	all passages	

Answer Sheet

page _____

1. Ⓐ Ⓑ Ⓒ Ⓓ
2. Ⓐ Ⓑ Ⓒ Ⓓ
3. Ⓐ Ⓑ Ⓒ Ⓓ
4. Ⓐ Ⓑ Ⓒ Ⓓ
5. Ⓐ Ⓑ Ⓒ Ⓓ

page _____

1. Ⓐ Ⓑ Ⓒ Ⓓ
2. Ⓐ Ⓑ Ⓒ Ⓓ
3. Ⓐ Ⓑ Ⓒ Ⓓ
4. Ⓐ Ⓑ Ⓒ Ⓓ
5. Ⓐ Ⓑ Ⓒ Ⓓ

page _____

1. Ⓐ Ⓑ Ⓒ Ⓓ
2. Ⓐ Ⓑ Ⓒ Ⓓ
3. Ⓐ Ⓑ Ⓒ Ⓓ
4. Ⓐ Ⓑ Ⓒ Ⓓ
5. Ⓐ Ⓑ Ⓒ Ⓓ

page _____

1. Ⓐ Ⓑ Ⓒ Ⓓ
2. Ⓐ Ⓑ Ⓒ Ⓓ
3. Ⓐ Ⓑ Ⓒ Ⓓ
4. Ⓐ Ⓑ Ⓒ Ⓓ
5. Ⓐ Ⓑ Ⓒ Ⓓ

page _____

1. Ⓐ Ⓑ Ⓒ Ⓓ
2. Ⓐ Ⓑ Ⓒ Ⓓ
3. Ⓐ Ⓑ Ⓒ Ⓓ
4. Ⓐ Ⓑ Ⓒ Ⓓ
5. Ⓐ Ⓑ Ⓒ Ⓓ

page _____

1. Ⓐ Ⓑ Ⓒ Ⓓ
2. Ⓐ Ⓑ Ⓒ Ⓓ
3. Ⓐ Ⓑ Ⓒ Ⓓ
4. Ⓐ Ⓑ Ⓒ Ⓓ
5. Ⓐ Ⓑ Ⓒ Ⓓ

page _____

1. Ⓐ Ⓑ Ⓒ Ⓓ
2. Ⓐ Ⓑ Ⓒ Ⓓ
3. Ⓐ Ⓑ Ⓒ Ⓓ
4. Ⓐ Ⓑ Ⓒ Ⓓ
5. Ⓐ Ⓑ Ⓒ Ⓓ

page _____

1. Ⓐ Ⓑ Ⓒ Ⓓ
2. Ⓐ Ⓑ Ⓒ Ⓓ
3. Ⓐ Ⓑ Ⓒ Ⓓ
4. Ⓐ Ⓑ Ⓒ Ⓓ
5. Ⓐ Ⓑ Ⓒ Ⓓ

page _____

1. Ⓐ Ⓑ Ⓒ Ⓓ
2. Ⓐ Ⓑ Ⓒ Ⓓ
3. Ⓐ Ⓑ Ⓒ Ⓓ
4. Ⓐ Ⓑ Ⓒ Ⓓ
5. Ⓐ Ⓑ Ⓒ Ⓓ

page _____

1. Ⓐ Ⓑ Ⓒ Ⓓ
2. Ⓐ Ⓑ Ⓒ Ⓓ
3. Ⓐ Ⓑ Ⓒ Ⓓ
4. Ⓐ Ⓑ Ⓒ Ⓓ
5. Ⓐ Ⓑ Ⓒ Ⓓ

page _____

1. Ⓐ Ⓑ Ⓒ Ⓓ
2. Ⓐ Ⓑ Ⓒ Ⓓ
3. Ⓐ Ⓑ Ⓒ Ⓓ
4. Ⓐ Ⓑ Ⓒ Ⓓ
5. Ⓐ Ⓑ Ⓒ Ⓓ

page _____

1. Ⓐ Ⓑ Ⓒ Ⓓ
2. Ⓐ Ⓑ Ⓒ Ⓓ
3. Ⓐ Ⓑ Ⓒ Ⓓ
4. Ⓐ Ⓑ Ⓒ Ⓓ
5. Ⓐ Ⓑ Ⓒ Ⓓ

page _____

1. Ⓐ Ⓑ Ⓒ Ⓓ
2. Ⓐ Ⓑ Ⓒ Ⓓ
3. Ⓐ Ⓑ Ⓒ Ⓓ
4. Ⓐ Ⓑ Ⓒ Ⓓ
5. Ⓐ Ⓑ Ⓒ Ⓓ

page _____

1. Ⓐ Ⓑ Ⓒ Ⓓ
2. Ⓐ Ⓑ Ⓒ Ⓓ
3. Ⓐ Ⓑ Ⓒ Ⓓ
4. Ⓐ Ⓑ Ⓒ Ⓓ
5. Ⓐ Ⓑ Ⓒ Ⓓ

page _____

1. Ⓐ Ⓑ Ⓒ Ⓓ
2. Ⓐ Ⓑ Ⓒ Ⓓ
3. Ⓐ Ⓑ Ⓒ Ⓓ
4. Ⓐ Ⓑ Ⓒ Ⓓ
5. Ⓐ Ⓑ Ⓒ Ⓓ

Panda, the Guide Horse

Ann is blind. Ann has a guide that helps her work and get around. Ann's guide stops at curbs. The guide leads Ann across busy streets when it is safe. The guide touches door handles so Ann can find them. The guide gets in cars and rides on trains. The guide goes with Ann into grocery stores and on picnics. The guide picks up keys or other things Ann drops. Who is this guide? It is a horse! It is a real, live, miniature horse!

Ann's miniature horse guide is called Panda. Panda's coat is black and white. Like other horses, Panda has a long thick mane and tail. Unlike other horses, Panda is quite small. She only stands 29 inches (74 cm) at the shoulder. She only weighs about 120 pounds (54 kg).

Panda stays with Ann at her house. Ann is a teacher, and Panda goes with Ann to Ann's school when Ann is working. Panda knows where every room is in the school. Panda rings a special bell when she needs to go to the bathroom. The bell is tied to a door. When Panda rings the bell, Panda is taken to a special area where she can relieve herself.

DO NOT TOUCH

A Horse Lesson in Good Manners

Boys and girls, you need to learn some good manners! You need to learn proper behavior! My name is Toby. I am a miniature horse. I work as a guide. I work hard helping someone who cannot see.

I had a special trainer. The trainer trained me by clicking a clicker. When I did something right, she clicked the clicker and gave me food as a reward. I was never punished. My trainer taught me how to use stairs. She taught me how to get into cars. Do you know what the hardest thing she taught me was? It was not using stairs or getting into a car. It was learning how to wait. It is very hard to wait. It is very hard to stand and do nothing.

I learned how to do something hard, so I know you can learn how to do something hard, too. You must learn not to touch me without asking. It is not good manners to touch me when I am working. I am working even when I am waiting. If I am petted, I do not know if I am still working. I might think it is time to play. Then I might have a hard time getting back to work.

Show What You Know

Answer the questions on "Panda, the Guide Horse" and "A Horse Lesson in Good Manners." You may look back at what you have read if you need to.

1. **Where does Ann work?**
   - Ⓐ on a train
   - Ⓑ at a picnic
   - Ⓒ at a school
   - Ⓓ at a grocery store

2. **What was the hardest thing for Toby to learn?**
   - Ⓐ how to wait
   - Ⓑ how to use stairs
   - Ⓒ how to get into a car
   - Ⓓ how to listen to a clicker

3. **Both stories are about**
   - Ⓐ the manners of miniature horses.
   - Ⓑ Ann and her guides Toby and Panda.
   - Ⓒ miniature horse guides for the blind.
   - Ⓓ how miniature guide horses are trained.

4. **From the stories one can tell that guide horses**
   - Ⓐ must be able to fit in cars.
   - Ⓑ must be able to click a clicker.
   - Ⓒ must be able to open doors with keys.
   - Ⓓ must be able to teach proper behavior.

5. **A fiction story is made up. It is not a true story. "A Horse Lesson in Good Manners" is fiction. You can tell the story is fiction because**
   - Ⓐ horses cannot use stairs.
   - Ⓑ horses cannot tell stories.
   - Ⓒ horses cannot get into cars.
   - Ⓓ horses cannot be trained using a clicker.

Show What You Know (cont.)

6. **List four things that Panda was trained to do.**

   1. _____

   2. _____

   3. _____

   4. _____

7. **Fill in the blanks that you can. One blank cannot be filled in.**

   What was the hardest thing Toby learned to do? _____

   Where was Toby trained? _____

   When was Toby punished? _____

   Why was Toby trained? _____

   How was Toby trained? _____

Write two or more sentences that tell what each story is about.

8. **"Panda, the Guide Horse"** _____

   _____

9. **"A Horse Lesson in Good Manners"** _____

   _____

10. **Guide dogs do the same job as guide horses. Write how you think you should act around a guide dog. Tell why.**

    _____

    _____

    _____

Walking on the Ocean

David Hempleman-Adams walked on the ocean. He walked to the top of the world. He walked to the North Pole. The North Pole is not on land. It is in the center of the Arctic Ocean. The Arctic Ocean is very cold. At times, parts of it are frozen solid. When David walked to the North Pole, he walked on the frozen ocean. He walked on ice.

David went with a partner. Both David and his partner used skis. They pulled sledges. Sledges are large, heavy sleds. The sledges held all of their equipment. It was hard to pull their sledges across the ice. This was because the ice was not one solid, smooth sheet. The ice was a bunch of broken ice floes. Some of the floes had smashed together. Others had drifted apart.

One time, David fell into the water when he was crossing from one floe to another. His partner saved him. Back on the ice, David's pants froze solid. There was no place to change clothes. There was no place to dry off. David had to keep on skiing in his frozen pants. This was so his body warmth would dry his clothes from the inside. If David had stopped, he would have died.

The House that Grandpa Built

Grandpa built a house. The house was not made of wood or straw. It was not made of bricks or stones. It was not made of clay or mud. Grandpa's house was made of snow. Snow is cold, but people in Grandpa's house stayed warm. How could this be?

Grandpa built an igloo. Long ago, people in the far north built igloos. Igloos are constructed with blocks of snow. Snow is cold, but the igloos were like blankets. You use blankets to keep you warm at night. Your blankets don't make heat, but they do two things. First, the blankets keep the heat your body gives off close to you. Second, the blankets keep the cold, outside air away from you.

Igloos are constructed from blocks of snow. The blocks are pressed tightly together. The blocks of snow are packed so tightly that it is hard for air to pass through them. The blocks keep inside air from leaking out. They keep outside air from getting in. People inside the igloo warm the air with their body heat. They warm the air as they cook their food. The warm air stays inside the igloo. It cannot escape through the tightly packed blocks of snow.

Show What You Know

Answer the questions on "Walking on the Ocean" and "The House that Grandpa Built." You may look back at what you have read if you need to.

1. **What is *not* true about the North Pole?**
   - Ⓐ It is on land.
   - Ⓑ It is in a cold place.
   - Ⓒ It is hard to walk to.
   - Ⓓ It is in the center of an ocean.

2. **Igloos were constructed in the**
   - Ⓐ far east.
   - Ⓑ far west.
   - Ⓒ far north.
   - Ⓓ far south.

3. **What do both stories have in common?**
   - Ⓐ skiing in a cold place
   - Ⓑ doing something in a cold place
   - Ⓒ pulling sledges in a cold place
   - Ⓓ building a place to stay in a cold place

4. **From the stories you can tell that**
   - Ⓐ our bodies keep air out.
   - Ⓑ our bodies give off heat.
   - Ⓒ our bodies are like blankets.
   - Ⓓ our bodies are tightly packed.

5. **Most likely, people built igloos because**
   - Ⓐ they did not have any blankets.
   - Ⓑ they needed a place to dry off.
   - Ⓒ they could pull the snow on a sledge.
   - Ⓓ there was more snow than stones or wood.

14

Show What You Know (cont.)

6. **Circle the word that is wrong. Write the correct word.**

   David went to the South Pole. _____

   The Indian Ocean is very cold. _____

   The sledges were very light. _____

   If David had stopped, he would have slept. _____

7. **List the two ways an igloo is like a blanket.**

   1. _____

   _____

   2. _____

   _____

Write two or more sentences that tell what each story is about.

8. **"Walking on the Ocean"** _____

   _____

9. **"The House that Grandpa Built"** _____

   _____

10. **When David Hempleman-Adams went to the North Pole, he slept in a tent. Why would a tent be better than an igloo? Why would an igloo be better than a tent?**

    _____

    _____

    _____

Danger! Do Not Band! Danger!

Scientists band birds. When scientists catch birds, they carefully place bands on the birds' legs. The bands are small and light. They have numbers. The banded birds are then released. The bands help the scientists keep track of where the birds go. They help them keep track of how many birds there are.

Scientists learned the hard way that some birds shouldn't be banded. Condors are big birds. Condors are among the biggest flying birds in the world. Condors shouldn't be banded. Banding condors is very dangerous. It's so dangerous it can cause the bird to grow very ill and die. Other birds are not harmed by being banded. Why is it so dangerous for the condor?

When condors are hot, they cool themselves in a special way. They cool themselves by going to the bathroom on their legs. As their waste dries, it cools their blood. When a condor is banded, the waste collects around the band. It builds up. It glues the band to the bird's leg.

When this happens, the condor's leg can get infected. The condor can become ill and die. Today, scientists do not use bands to track condors. They use radio tags. The radio tags are put on the condors' wings near the shoulder.

Shing and the World Record Holder

One morning, Shing went for a walk on the rocks along the ocean shore. Suddenly, Shing saw something. Shing ran close and saw that it was bird. The bird was caught in some fishing line. It was struggling to free itself. Shing ran and got the park ranger. "Come quickly," said Shing. "A bird is caught in some fishing line. It is struggling to free itself. I think the line needs to be cut. Please come quickly."

Shing led the park ranger to the bird. The park ranger very carefully cut away the fishing line from the struggling bird. Before the park ranger released the bird, she did something. She looked at a band on the bird's leg. She carefully wrote down the number, the date, and where the bird was found. Only then did she let the bird go.

The park ranger told Shing, "This bird is an arctic tern. The arctic tern holds a world record. It holds the world record for how far it migrates. The bird flies from the Arctic Circle. It flies to the Antarctic Circle. It flies halfway around the world. It goes back and forth every year. No other bird migrates so far. How did scientists learn this? They learned it by banding birds."

Show What You Know

Answer the questions on "Danger! Do Not Band! Danger!" and "Shing and the World Record Holder." You may look back at what you have read if you need to.

1. **Scientists keep track of condors**
   - Ⓐ by banding them.
   - Ⓑ by using radio tags.
   - Ⓒ by gluing a band to their legs.
   - Ⓓ by cooling them in a special way.

2. **The arctic tern holds a world record**
   - Ⓐ for being banded.
   - Ⓑ for how far it migrates.
   - Ⓒ for going back and forth.
   - Ⓓ for flying to the Arctic Circle.

3. **What do both stories have in common?**
   - Ⓐ They both are about finding birds.
   - Ⓑ They both are about releasing birds.
   - Ⓒ They both are about migrating birds.
   - Ⓓ They both are about keeping track of birds.

4. **Most likely, scientists learned not to band condors**
   - Ⓐ when some condors' legs got infected.
   - Ⓑ when they could not track the condors.
   - Ⓒ when some condors got caught in fishing line.
   - Ⓓ when they learned how condors cool themselves.

5. **Most likely, a radio tag was not used on the arctic tern because**
   - Ⓐ a band is lighter.
   - Ⓑ a tern flies farther than a condor.
   - Ⓒ a band does not cause the tern harm.
   - Ⓓ a tern's wings are not as big as a condor's.

Show What You Know (cont.)

6. **List what information you learned about the two birds in the stories.**

Condors	Arctic Terns
1.	1.
2.	2.
3.	3.

7. **Think about when things happened in the story. Fill in the boxes to show what order they happened in the story.**

1.	2. Shing saw bird.	3.
4. Park ranger cut fishing line.	5.	6. Bird is released.

Write two or more sentences that tell what each story is about.

8. **"Danger! Do Not Band! Danger!"** _____

   _____

9. **"Shing and the World Record Holder"** _____

   _____

10. **Should all, some, or no birds be banded? Tell why or why not. Use examples from the stories in your answer.**

    _____

    _____

    _____

What the Insects Proved

The police said, "We know he did it. The man is guilty. We need to prove it." The man was sure no one could prove his guilt. This was because the crime took place far away. It took place in California. The man was in Ohio. The man said he was in Ohio when the crime took place. But was he?

The man had a new rental car. No one else had driven the car. The police said the man could have driven all night. He could have driven to California. He could have driven back. The man said he didn't. He said he had never left Ohio.

The police took the car to an entomologist. An entomologist studies insects. The entomologist worked hard. She picked out insects and insect parts from the car. It took over seven hours. Then she looked at the insects. She studied the parts. She figured out what kinds of insects they were.

What did the entomologist find? She found insects that are only found in California. This proved the man was lying. He had driven the car to California. In addition, the entomologist did not find any butterflies. Butterflies are insects that are out only in the day. The lack of butterflies meant that the car was driven at night.

The Identical Flowers

Cows were being let out. Horses were being let out. Pots were being turned over. People in the village wanted to stop the mischief. They were afraid to. This was because the mischief was being caused by a sprite.

The sprite came out at night. During the day, the sprite turned into a flower. The villagers could get rid of the sprite by digging up the flower, but they did not know which flower to dig up. There were ten flowers. The flowers were identical. They looked the same. If the villagers dug up the wrong flower, the village would disappear.

One day, an old man came to the village. The people were kind to the man. They fed him. As they took him to a soft bed to sleep in, the man said, "Show me the flowers in the morning."

The old man looked at the flowers the next morning. He said, "Dig this one up." The flowers were identical. They looked the same. How did the man know which one to dig up? The sprite was a sprite all night. It was a flower only in the day. The sprite was the only flower without dew on it.

Show What You Know

Answer the questions on "What the Insects Proved" and "The Identical Flowers."
You may look back at what you have read if you need to.

1. **How did the entomologist know the rental car was driven at night?**
   - Ⓐ She found butterfly parts on it.
   - Ⓑ She did not find butterfly parts on it.
   - Ⓒ She found insects found only in California on it.
   - Ⓓ She did not find insects found only in California on it.

2. **What would happen if the people in the village dug up the wrong flower?**
   - Ⓐ The sprite would disappear.
   - Ⓑ The old man would disappear.
   - Ⓒ The flowers would disappear.
   - Ⓓ The village would disappear.

3. **Both stories are about**
   - Ⓐ insect problems.
   - Ⓑ solving problems.
   - Ⓒ identical problems.
   - Ⓓ disappearing problems.

4. **The police needed to know what the entomologist told them. They also needed to know**
   - Ⓐ the car had no dew on it.
   - Ⓑ the car was not identical.
   - Ⓒ the car would not disappear.
   - Ⓓ no one else had driven the car.

5. **A fiction story is not real. It is made-up. You can tell that the story "The Identical Flowers" is fiction because**
   - Ⓐ sprites are not real.
   - Ⓑ dew is never found on flowers.
   - Ⓒ only entomologists know about sprites.
   - Ⓓ dew is only on flowers during the night.

22

Show What You Know (cont.)

6. **Complete the chart to show why it was important that the entomologist found or did not find what she did.**

	Found or Not Found	Proves
butterflies		
insects only from California		

7. **List in order what happened in the story. Use the numbers 1 to 5. The number 1 is by what happened first. Put 5 by what happened last.**

_____ pots turned over

_____ dew collected on flowers

___1___ sprite changed from flower to sprite

_____ old man looked at flowers

_____ sprite changed into flower

Write two or more sentences that tell what each story is about.

8. **"What the Insects Proved"** _____

_____

9. **"The Identical Flowers"** _____

_____

10. **Why might someone who grows flowers need the help of an entomologist?**

_____

_____

_____

Islands that Float

There are islands in Lake Titicaca. The islands are in the side of the lake by Peru. Peru is a country in South America. The islands float! How can this be?

The Uros people make the islands to live on. First, they cut down reeds. The reeds grow in the shallow waters of the lake. After the reeds are cut, they are laid in the sun to dry. Once they are dry, they are woven into mats. The mats are bound together. They are piled on top of each other. The mats form a floating island.

The Uros people use the reeds that grow in the lake for more than their islands. They use them to construct their homes, boats, and rafts. They also burn them, using them as fuel. The reeds' soft parts are eaten like a vegetable, and the reeds' flowers are boiled to make a healing tea.

What is it like to walk on the man-made islands? The ground feels soft and spongy. Sometimes the ground gives way! The reed mats rot away! What do the Uros people do? They pile on more mats. They keep adding layers of fresh dry reeds as the old reeds rot.

Silly Rudolph

Silly Rudolph went to Lake Titicaca. He visited the Uros people on a floating island. When Rudolph saw the reed houses on the island, he said, "These people are silly! Don't they know brick houses are better? Brick houses will not rot. They will not fall down. I will make a brick house. I will show these silly people how to construct a proper house."

Rudolph went and got some bricks. The bricks cost a lot of money. Rudolph took the bricks to the island. It took many boat trips. Finally, when Rudolph had enough bricks, he began to build his house. It took a long time. When Rudolph was done, he called everyone over. He said, "This is the best house. This house will not rot. It will last a long time."

Just then, the brick house sank! It was too heavy for the floating island. It sank deep under the water. It left a hole in the island. Rudolph was very surprised. "Oh!" Rudolph said, "The best houses are not made of brick! They are made of reeds! I will go back home. I will go back to windy, snowy Wisconsin. I will show the people there how to make a light, reed house."

Show What You Know

Answer the questions on "Islands that Float" and "Silly Rudolph."
You may look back at what you have read if you need to.

1. **To make an island from reeds, the reeds are first cut. Next, they are**
   - (A) bound together.
   - (B) woven into mats.
   - (C) laid in the sun to dry.
   - (D) piled on top of each other.

2. **Why did Silly Rudolph think a brick house was best?**
   - (A) It would not rot.
   - (B) It would not sink.
   - (C) It would not cost a lot.
   - (D) It would not be easy to build.

3. **What do both stories have in common?**
   - (A) making islands that float
   - (B) houses for the Uros people
   - (C) sinking deep under the water
   - (D) islands found in Peru and Wisconsin

4. **Most likely, the Uros people use reeds to construct their islands because**
   - (A) the reeds cost a lot.
   - (B) the reeds are very heavy.
   - (C) the reeds grow in the lake.
   - (D) the reeds rot in the water.

5. **What did Silly Rudolph need to learn?**
   - (A) No proper houses are made of brick.
   - (B) All proper houses are made of reeds.
   - (C) All proper houses are constructed in the same way.
   - (D) Not all proper houses are constructed in the same way.

Show What You Know (cont.)

6. **List all the things for which the Uros people use the reeds that grow in the lake.**

1. _____   4. _____   7. _____

2. _____   5. _____

3. _____   6. _____

7. **Fill in the chart using the words "yes" or "no."**

	reeds	bricks
easy to get		
heavy		
can rot		
easy to add on		

Write two or more sentences that tell what each story is about.

8. **"Islands that Float"** _____

_____

9. **"Silly Rudolph"** _____

_____

10. **Do you think a reed house would be a proper house for Wisconsin? Tell why or why not.**

_____

_____

_____

The Pilot's Problem

Jackie Cochran wanted to get her pilot's license. She had taken lessons. She knew how to fly. All that was left was a written test. The written test was a problem. Jackie was very smart. She was a hard worker. She could fly any plane. The problem was that Jackie could barely read and write.

Jackie was born in 1912. When Jackie was little, she did not live with her real family. The people she lived with did not take good care of her. Jackie often went hungry. She was not sent to school. Jackie had worked hard to learn how to fly. She wasn't going to let her lack of education stop her.

Jackie asked to take the test orally. An oral test is a spoken test. Someone read the test to Jackie. Jackie answered out loud. Jackie passed with the highest score.

Jackie set many speed and distance records in her lifetime. She even flew faster than the speed of sound! One time, Jackie's plane caught on fire. Smoke filled the cabin. Jackie could barely see the landing strip. Jackie calmly radioed for fire trucks. She jumped out of the plane seconds before it crashed. The plane and the grass landing strip burned up. Jackie was fine. Her calm actions had saved her.

How Marshall Knew

Marshall was babysitting his younger brother Dakota. Marshall said, "I have read you six stories. Now it is time to go to sleep. I am turning out the light."

Dakota said, "No! No! I don't want to go to sleep. I want to hear more stories. If you will not read to me, I will read to myself."

Marshall did not think that Dakota could read yet. Dakota was only four. Dakota only went to preschool. Marshall said, "Dakota, one day you will learn how to read like me. For now, you will just have to go to sleep."

Dakota said, "I don't care if you don't read to me. I can read. Just listen." Marshall listened. He listened as Dakota turned the pages of a book and said, "The Story of Jackie Cochran. Jackie was a little girl. She was very poor. She only went to school for two years. She started working when she was eight years old. When she grew up, she flew planes."

Marshall said, "Dakota, you are not reading. You are only saying out loud what you have heard me say many times."

Dakota said, "How do you know I'm not really reading?"

Marshall said, "You are holding the book upside down!"

Show What You Know

Answer the questions on "The Pilot's Problem" and "How Marshall Knew."
You may look back at what you have read if you need to.

1. **Jackie asked to take the test orally because**
   - (A) she could barely read and write.
   - (B) she passed with the highest score.
   - (C) she set many speed and distance records.
   - (D) she flew faster than the speed of sound.

2. **How old was Dakota?**
   - (A) 2
   - (B) 4
   - (C) 6
   - (D) 8

3. **What do both stories have in common?**
   - (A) people who write
   - (B) people who babysit
   - (C) people who take tests
   - (D) people who cannot read well

4. **Jackie's learning to fly shows us that**
   - (A) no one needs to learn how to read.
   - (B) only people who can read know things.
   - (C) the best pilots can read upside down.
   - (D) people can learn even if they can't read.

5. **Dakota could only say the things he did about Jackie Cochran because**
   - (A) he was calm.
   - (B) he knew how to read.
   - (C) he had heard them orally.
   - (D) he could read upside down.

Show What You Know (cont.)

6. **List in order what happened in the story. Use the numbers 1 to 5. Put 1 by what happened first. Put 5 by what happened last.**

    _____ took test orally

    _____ lives with family who didn't care for her

    _____ set distance record

    _____ born in 1912

    _____ learned to fly

7. **Try to read this sentence:**

    Jackie Cochran was the first woman to fly faster than the speed of sound.

    Now, turn the page over and read the sentence again. Put a check by what way the sentence was easier to read.

    _____ upside down   _____ right side up

Write two or more sentences that tell what each story is about.

8. **"The Pilot's Problem"** _____

    _____

9. **"How Marshall Knew"** _____

    _____

10. **Do you think it is easier to do well in this world if you can read? Tell why or why not.**

Why Astronauts Have Puffy Faces

Astronauts go into space. In space, something happens to the astronauts' faces. Their faces become puffy. Why do their faces become puffy? It is because of weightlessness. In space, fluids shift upward. Our bodies are filled with fluids. Fluids are liquids. The fluids inside an astronaut's body shift upward. They rise up to the face.

Early astronauts could not spice their food. They could not use salt or pepper. This was because of weightlessness. Salt and pepper were in the form of a grain. The salt and pepper grains could float away. It could make problems. It could bother the astronauts. It could float into their noses. It could float into parts of the ship.

Today astronauts can use salt and pepper. This is because the salt and pepper have been changed. They have been changed into a different form. They are no longer in the form of a grain. They are in the form of a liquid.

Astronauts are in space for many days. They have to sleep. Most astronauts sleep less soundly in space. They keep waking up. This is because the space shuttle circles the Earth. It circles the Earth about 16 times in 24 hours. This means astronauts see 16 sunrises in one day! They see 16 sunsets!

Vacation Journal 2022

May 5, 2022

Dear Journal,

I am on vacation! We left our spaceship home. We landed on a planet. The planet is Earth. It is very strange on Earth. It is strange because things fall! Yes, it is hard to believe, but I am telling the truth. If you let go of something on Earth, it falls to the ground. It does not float. This is because of Earth's gravity. If something is lost on Earth, it is probably easy to find. This is because it just stays on the ground. It stays in one place. It does not float around the way it does on our spaceship.

~~~~~~

June 15, 2022

Dear Journal,

I am back from vacation. I am back on our spaceship. Did you know that on vacation I shrunk? I lost two inches (5 cm)! This was because of that gravity thing again. Mom says not to worry. She says I'll get my height back. This is because there is less pressure on my spine in our spaceship. This is because gravity isn't a problem here. Here, my spine can spring back to normal. Earth was fun, but it is good to be back on our spaceship home.

Show What You Know

Answer the questions on "Why Astronauts Have Puffy Faces" and "Vacation Journal 2022." You may look back at what you have read if you need to.

1. **In space, fluids**
   Ⓐ do not shift.
   Ⓑ shift upward.
   Ⓒ shift sideways.
   Ⓓ shift downward.

2. **Why did the person writing the journal think it would be easy to find things on Earth?**
   Ⓐ On Earth, things shrink.
   Ⓑ On Earth, things moved around.
   Ⓒ On Earth, things have less pressure.
   Ⓓ On Earth, things did not float around.

3. **Both stories are about what happens**
   Ⓐ when one is and isn't an astronaut.
   Ⓑ when one's face is and isn't puffy.
   Ⓒ when one is and isn't on a spaceship.
   Ⓓ when one's salt and pepper is a liquid form.

4. **From the stories, you can tell that one feels weightlessness**
   Ⓐ when there is little gravity.
   Ⓑ when there is a lot of fluids.
   Ⓒ when one is on the planet Earth.
   Ⓓ when one is in the form of a grain.

5. **From the journal, you can tell that the person who wrote it**
   Ⓐ was very tall.
   Ⓑ saw 16 sunrises in a day.
   Ⓒ ate salt and pepper in a liquid form.
   Ⓓ thought living on a spaceship was normal.

Show What You Know (cont.)

6. **Circle which ones are fluids on Earth.**

   water   bread   banana   tea

   salt   apple juice   orange juice   pepper

7. **Write "float" or "drop" to show what would most likely happen to a pencil if the person who wrote the journal dropped it on**

   May 4 _____   June 4 _____

   May 10 _____   June 10 _____

   May 20 _____   June 20 _____

Write two or more sentences that tell what each story is about.

8. **"Why Astronauts Have Puffy Faces"** _____

   _____

9. **"Vacation Journal 2022"** _____

   _____

10. **What do you think happens to an astronaut's height when he or she lives on the space shuttle? Tell why you think so.**

    _____

    _____

    _____

The Beetles that Ride

A forest mouse scampers around. The mouse is deep in a rain forest. The rain forest is in Costa Rica. The mouse is scampering around in the night. It is looking for food.

There are beetles on the forest mouse. The beetles cling to the mouse's fur. They cling to the mouse's face. The beetles are riding on the mouse as it scampers through the rain forest. Does the mouse want to get rid of the beetles that are clinging on to its fur and face? Does the mouse want to get rid of the beetles that are catching a ride?

The mouse does not want to get rid of the beetles because of what the beetles are eating. What are the beetles eating? They are eating fleas on the mouse! The fleas live in the mouse's fur. The beetles are helping the mouse by keeping it clean.

At the end of the night, the forest mouse goes to its burrow. It sleeps during the day. The beetles get off of the mouse. They walk all around the mouse's burrow. They eat every flea they find. They eat other bugs, too. The beetles clean the burrow as the mouse sleeps.

36

Melissa and the Leaves

Melissa could not play. She had to work. Melissa had to rake up all the leaves. Melissa didn't want to work, but she had to do what she was told. Just then, Melissa's friend Kamala came over. Kamala said, "It is too bad that you have to work. I was going to ask you to play."

Melissa smiled. She made herself look happy. She danced around with her rake. "Work?" she cried! "What makes you think raking leaves is work? This is fun! I am the luckiest girl alive! I get to rake leaves, and you don't!"

All of a sudden Kamala wanted to rake leaves, too. "Okay," said Melissa. "I am only going to let you have fun raking leaves because you are my friend."

While Kamala was working, more of Melissa's friends came to watch. Melissa told her friends they could not rake leaves and have fun. This made Melissa's friends want to rake leaves, too. They begged Melissa to be allowed a turn. Pretty soon all the leaves were raked. Melissa had not worked at all, but the work was done. When Melissa's friends told Melissa that they had fun, Melissa said, "I did, too."

Show What You Know

Answer the questions on "The Beetles that Ride" and "Melissa and the Leaves."
You may look back at what you have read if you need to.

1. **The mouse does not want to get rid of the beetles that cling to it because the beetles**
   - (A) get off during the night.
   - (B) help the mouse stay clean.
   - (C) help the mouse look for food.
   - (D) get a ride through the rain forest.

2. **What did Melissa do?**
   - (A) She raked up the leaves.
   - (B) She played with her friends.
   - (C) She begged to be allowed a turn.
   - (D) She made her friends want to work.

3. **What do both stories have in common?**
   - (A) They are both about getting a ride.
   - (B) They are both about leaves in Costa Rica.
   - (C) They are both about one doing work for another.
   - (D) They are both about friends that cling or dance.

4. **What answer is *not* true?**
   - (A) Melissa helped her friends work.
   - (B) Melissa's friends helped Melissa work.
   - (C) The mouse helps the beetles with food.
   - (D) The beetles help the mouse with cleaning.

5. **Most likely, Kamala would not have wanted to rake leaves if she thought that**
   - (A) raking leaves was work.
   - (B) leaves were clinging to her.
   - (C) she was the luckiest girl alive.
   - (D) Melissa's other friends would want to rake them, too.

Show What You Know (cont.)

6. **List in the boxes what beetles do during the**

Day	Night

7. **List in order what happens in the story. Use the numbers 1 to 6. Put 1 by what happened first. Put 6 by what happened last.**

_____ Kamala raked the leaves.

_____ All the leaves were raked.

_____ Melissa made more friends think raking leaves was fun.

_____ Melissa makes Kamala think raking leaves is fun.

_____ Kamala came over.

_____ Other friends came over.

Write two or more sentences that tell what each story is about.

8. **"The Beetles that Ride"** _____

_____

9. **"Melissa and the Leaves"** _____

_____

10. **Think about the beetles, the mouse, Melissa, and Kamala. Who do you think got the most and gave the least? Tell why or why not.**

_____

_____

_____

The President's Ticket

Ulysses Grant was President of the United States. He was President from 1869 to 1877. He was the 18th President.

Presidents work hard. They work a lot. They work many hours. Still, Presidents need some time off. They need time to relax. When Grant was President, he did something to relax. He would drive himself around Washington. He would drive all around the city.

Grant would drive himself in a gig. A gig is a carriage. It is very light. It has just two wheels. It is pulled by just one horse. One day, Grant was driving on M Street. Grant was speeding. He was driving his gig too fast.

A policeman saw Grant speeding. The policeman stopped Grant. The policeman did not know who was driving the gig. He did not know that he had stopped the President. The policeman gave Grant a speeding ticket. The fine for speeding was 25 dollars. This was a lot of money at that time!

What did Grant do when he got the ticket? He did two things. First, he paid the fine. He paid the 25 dollars. Second, he commended the policeman for writing the ticket. When someone is commended, they are praised. They are told they acted well. They are told they did a good thing.

The Neighbor Who Didn't Get a Ticket

Mr. Swan said, "We have rules to keep us safe. For example, we have traffic rules. One rule is that you must stop at a red light. You must also stop at a stop sign. These rules keep us safe. They stop accidents. They stop cars from crashing into each other. Police officers give tickets to people who do not obey the rules. The people who get tickets have to pay a fine."

Lori said, "My neighbor runs red lights all the time. When he comes to an intersection, he does not wait his turn. He races right through. He goes through the intersection without stopping."

Mr. Swan said, "Lori, this is not good. Your neighbor should stop at red lights and stop signs. He should not race through intersections. He is going to cause accidents. Police officers are going to give him tickets. Your neighbor is going to have to pay fines."

Lori said, "Police officers give tickets to people who get in the way of my neighbor! This is because my neighbor is a firefighter. He races to fires. He races to accidents. He races through intersections so he can help people. He puts on a siren so people know he is coming."

Show What You Know

Answer the questions on "The President's Ticket" and "The Neighbor Who Didn't Get a Ticket." You may look back at what you have read if you need to.

1. **Grant commended the policeman because**
   - Ⓐ the policeman drove a gig.
   - Ⓑ the policeman praised the President.
   - Ⓒ the policeman gave him a ticket for speeding.
   - Ⓓ the policeman did not know he had stopped the President.

2. **Mr. Swan said, "Your neighbor should stop at red lights and stop signs." When Mr. Swan said this,**
   - Ⓐ he did not think about accidents.
   - Ⓑ he did not know what Lori's neighbor did.
   - Ⓒ he did not want Lori's neighbor to pay a fine.
   - Ⓓ he did not think Lori's neighbor should obey the rules.

3. **What do both stories have in common?**
   - Ⓐ They both are about being commended.
   - Ⓑ They both are about people who paid fines.
   - Ⓒ They both are about going through intersections.
   - Ⓓ They both are about getting tickets for speeding.

4. **From the stories, you can tell that**
   - Ⓐ people crashed more in the 1800s.
   - Ⓑ there were traffic rules in the 1800s.
   - Ⓒ fire trucks did not use sirens in the 1800s.
   - Ⓓ fines today are more than they were in the 1800s.

5. **A firefighter would have to pay a speeding fine**
   - Ⓐ if he or she was speeding on M Street.
   - Ⓑ if he or she raced through an intersection.
   - Ⓒ if he or she was in a fire truck with its siren on.
   - Ⓓ if he or she was speeding when he or she wasn't working.

Show What You Know (cont.)

6. Circle the gig.

Answer these questions to check your answer.

A gig has how many wheels? _____

A gig is pulled by how many horses? _____

7. People talked in one story. List who talked in the story.

1st _____

2nd _____

3rd _____

4th _____

Write two or more sentences that tell what each story is about.

8. "The President's Ticket " _____

_____

9. "The Neighbor Who Didn't Get a Ticket" _____

_____

10. Think about the police officer who gave the president a ticket. Do you think that police officer would give a ticket to Lori's neighbor? Tell why or why not and when.

_____

_____

_____

Gorilla Hero

It was Friday afternoon. A three-year-old boy was at the zoo in Chicago. He was looking at gorillas. The gorillas were in a display area. The display area was surrounded by a stone wall. The stone wall had a rail. The boy climbed up on the stone wall. He lost his balance. He fell over the rail. He fell down into the display area. He fell 20 feet (6 m). He was knocked unconscious.

People screamed in fear. They called for help. They were afraid the gorillas would harm the boy. A mother gorilla named Binti Jua got to the boy first. Binti was eight years old. Binti Jua's own baby clung to her back. Binti Jua carefully picked up the unconscious boy. She began to walk with him. She carried him in her arms. Other gorillas came close. Binti Jua turned her back to the other gorillas. She protected the boy with her body.

Binti Jua walked to a door. It was a service door. Binti Jua knew this was a door where keepers could enter. Binti Jua carefully put the limp boy down. She waited until people came. She kept the boy safe. Binti Jua was a good mother. She was a hero.

Gorilla Day

Mrs. Ray said, "Class, we have finished our gorilla lesson. We have learned a lot. We learned that gorillas are the largest apes. We learned that they do not eat meat. They eat plants. We learned that each gorilla has a nose print. A gorilla's nose print is like our fingerprint. No two are the same.

"Class, we had fun with the lesson. Now we will have fun with riddles. I will ask you four riddles. You will figure out the answers. The first riddle is about months. 'In what month of the year do gorillas have the most fun?' The second riddle is about time. 'What time is it when a gorilla sits on your watch?' The third riddle is, 'What do gorillas eat for lunch?' The fourth riddle is, 'Why did the gorilla walk up the stairs?'"

Mrs. Ray's students liked the riddles. They figured out the answers. The answer to the first riddle was, "Ape-ril (April)." The answer to the second riddle was, "Time to get a new watch." The answer to the third riddle was, "Go-rilled cheese sandwiches (grilled cheese sandwiches)." The answer to the fourth riddle was, "He couldn't fit in the elevator."

Mrs. Ray said, "Go-rilla time is over. Now it is Stop-rilla time."

Show What You Know

Answer the questions on "Gorilla Hero" and "Gorilla Day."
You may look back at what you have read if you need to.

1. **Where was Binti Jua's baby when she carried the boy?**
   - Ⓐ in her arms
   - Ⓑ by her side
   - Ⓒ on her back
   - Ⓓ by the door

2. **What is *not* true about gorillas?**
   - Ⓐ They eat meat.
   - Ⓑ They can be told apart.
   - Ⓒ They have a nose print.
   - Ⓓ They are the largest apes.

3. **Both stories are about**
   - Ⓐ heroes.
   - Ⓑ riddles.
   - Ⓒ lessons.
   - Ⓓ gorillas.

4. **From the stories one can tell that the gorillas**
   - Ⓐ told riddles after their lessons.
   - Ⓑ went in and out of the service door.
   - Ⓒ would not have thought the boy was food.
   - Ⓓ didn't have an elevator in the display area.

5. **The answer to the second riddle was "Time to get a new watch" because**
   - Ⓐ a gorilla doesn't wear a watch.
   - Ⓑ a gorilla's weight would break a watch.
   - Ⓒ a gorilla might lose its balance and fall.
   - Ⓓ a gorilla would put its nose on the watch.

Show What You Know (cont.)

6. **Think about when things happened in the story. Fill in the boxes to show when they happened in the story.**

1. Three-year-old boy was at Chicago zoo.	2.	3. Boy falls over rail.
4.	5. Binti Jua walked to service door.	6.

7. **Mrs. Ray told her class gorilla facts. Mrs. Ray told her class gorilla riddles. A fact is something true. A riddle is made-up. Write down a fact that Mrs. Ray said. Write down a riddle she said.**

Fact: _____

_____

Riddle: _____

_____

Write two or more sentences that tell what each story is about.

8. **"Gorilla Hero"** _____

_____

9. **"Gorilla Day"** _____

_____

10. **Pretend you were at the zoo the day Binti Jua saved the boy. Write down how you would feel as you watched everything happen. Did you ever feel like it was a time to tell riddles?**

_____

_____

_____

When Grandfather Yellowtail's Braids Could Snap

Joseph Medicine Crow was born in 1913. He was born on October 27th. Every morning, Joseph's grandfather Yellowtail would bathe. He would bathe in the spring. He would bathe in the summer. He would bathe in the fall. He would bathe in the winter. He would bathe in the Little Horn River that flowed past his house. Joseph would bathe, too.

In the winter, it would snow. Ice would cover the river. Joseph's grandfather would chop holes in the ice. He would water his horses. Then, he would bathe. He would get in the hole. He would go under the icy water. After he got out, he would pick up Joseph. He would dip Joseph in the icy water. Joseph's grandfather would hold tight to Joseph. He would not let go. This was because the current was strong. Grandfather did not want Joseph to be swept away under the ice.

Joseph and his grandfather would then walk back home. They would walk in the snow. They would get very cold. Grandfather wore his hair in two braids. On very cold mornings, his wet braids would freeze! They would become stiff and hard. If hit, they might snap off! Joseph's grandfather would carefully thaw out his braids to keep them safe.

Hot Water in the Snow

Dear Sara,

I am visiting Iceland.
Iceland is an island. It is
very cold here now. It is
the winter. Snow and ice
are everywhere. It is very
dark, too. This is because
Iceland is so close to the
Arctic Circle. Icelanders
are used to not seeing the

sun in the winter. My friend Ulla says that in the summer there is
lots of sun. She says it does not set for weeks!

You will not believe what Ulla and I did today. We went swimming
outside! We went swimming in the cold and the dark. We went
swimming in the cold, but we did not get cold. We were warm.
Why were we so warm? The water was heated. It was a hot spring.

Ulla says there are hot springs all over Iceland. A hot spring is
heated by natural heat. The heat comes from inside the earth. Hot
springs are heated by the same energy that makes volcanoes erupt!

Ulla and I pretended we were erupting volcanoes. We would burst
out of the hot water. We would splash hot water all over the icy
snow. It was fun. I wish you could have been here.

Your friend,

Tamara

Show What You Know

Answer the questions on "When Grandfather Yellowtail's Braids Could Snap" and "Hot Water in the Snow." You may look back at what you have read if you need to.

1. **Grandfather Yellowtail would hold tight to Joseph**
   - Ⓐ when he would thaw out Joseph's braids.
   - Ⓑ when he and Joseph would walk in the snow.
   - Ⓒ when he and Joseph would water the horses.
   - Ⓓ when he would dip Joseph in the icy water.

2. **Hot springs are heated by**
   - Ⓐ heat from the sun.
   - Ⓑ heat from inside the earth.
   - Ⓒ heat from the Arctic Circle.
   - Ⓓ heat from erupting volcanoes.

3. **Both stories are about**
   - Ⓐ getting in icy water.
   - Ⓑ getting in the water in winter.
   - Ⓒ getting in the water in a hot spring.
   - Ⓓ getting in water through a hole in the ice.

4. **You can tell that Grandfather did not bathe in a hot spring because**
   - Ⓐ he did not bathe outside.
   - Ⓑ he had to walk through snow.
   - Ⓒ he had to cut a hole in the ice.
   - Ⓓ he did not live by the Arctic Circle.

5. **When would Tamara's hair most likely freeze?**
   - Ⓐ before she got in the hot spring in the winter
   - Ⓑ after she got out of the hot spring in the summer
   - Ⓒ after she got out of the hot spring in the winter
   - Ⓓ before she got out of the hot spring in the summer

Show What You Know (cont.)

6. **Write down in order the things Grandfather Yellowtail would do after he chopped a hole in the ice.**

1.	2.	3. dip Joseph

4.	5. thaw out his braids

7. **If Tamara was writing a letter to Ulla, how would she start it?**

_____ _____ __

How would she end it?

_____ _____ __

_____

Write two or more sentences that tell what each story is about.

8. **"When Grandfather Yellowtail's Braids Could Snap"** _____

_____

9. **"Hot Water in the Snow"** _____

_____

10. **Do you think Tamara and Ulla would have gone swimming in the Little Horn River in the winter? Tell why or why not.**

_____

_____

_____

To Hold or Not to Hold

A rattlesnake bites a bird. A rattlesnake bites a rat. When the rattlesnake bites a bird, it holds on. It does not let go. When a rattlesnake bites a rat, it does not hold on. It lets the rat go. Why does the rattlesnake do this?

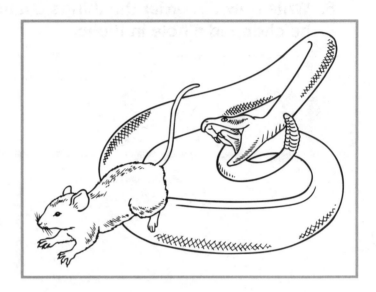

A rattlesnake is a poisonous snake. It has fangs. The fangs are hollow. When the rattlesnake bites, its fangs sink deep into its prey. Venom is pushed through the hollow fangs. It enters the prey. If the snake's prey is a bird, the snake must hold onto the bird. This is because the bird might fly away before the venom kills the bird.

If the rattlesnake's prey is a rat, the snake lets go. It waits for the venom to kill the rat. If the rat runs away, the snake follows it. The snake uses its tongue to pick up the rat's scent, or smell. A snake swallows its prey whole.

Rattlesnake venom is poisonous to birds and rats, but it is not poisonous to its enemy, the king snake. King snakes eat rattlesnakes. King snakes do not bite rattlesnakes, but they squeeze. They wrap themselves around a rattlesnake's body and do not let go. They hold on, squeezing hard, until the rattlesnake dies.

What Jillie Is Afraid Of

My name is Jillie. I am a rattlesnake. You humans have it all wrong. You humans are afraid of us rattlesnakes. You should not be. We do not want to bite you. We want to bite rats. We want to bite mice. We even want to bite poisonous scorpions! This is because we eat them. There would be a lot more pests around if it weren't for us rattlesnakes!

We are the only kind of snake with rattles. The rattles are at the end of our tails. Our rattles are made out of the same material as your fingernails. You cannot tell our age by the number of segments, or parts, our rattles are made of. You can only tell how many times we have shed our skin! I can start to rattle my tail after I have shed my skin at least once. I can add up to three segments in just one year.

You should not be afraid of our rattles. You should like us because we have rattles. Why should you like us? We shake our rattles to warn you! We shake our rattles so you will stay away! You are afraid of running into us, and we are afraid of running into you!

Show What You Know

Answer the questions on "To Hold or Not to Hold" and "What Jillie Is Afraid Of."
You may look back at what you have read if you need to.

1. **To smell, a rattlesnake**
   - Ⓐ uses its fangs.
   - Ⓑ uses its venom.
   - Ⓒ uses its scent.
   - Ⓓ uses its tongue.

2. **Most likely, if a rattlesnake cannot shake its rattle,**
   - Ⓐ it is three years old.
   - Ⓑ it is only one year old.
   - Ⓒ it has not shed its skin.
   - Ⓓ it can warn you to stay away.

3. **What do both stories have in common?**
   - Ⓐ what rattlesnakes eat
   - Ⓑ when rattlesnakes hold on
   - Ⓒ what rattlesnake venom is
   - Ⓓ why rattlesnakes have rattles

4. **Most likely, a rattlesnake holds onto a bird because**
   - Ⓐ rattlesnakes don't eat birds.
   - Ⓑ it might fly away too far to follow.
   - Ⓒ a bird cannot hear a rattlesnake's tail rattle.
   - Ⓓ a rattlesnake's venom is not poisonous to a bird.

5. **To Jillie, a poisonous scorpion is something**
   - Ⓐ to eat.
   - Ⓑ of a human.
   - Ⓒ to squeeze.
   - Ⓓ to be afraid of.

Show What You Know (cont.)

6. **Show what eats what.**

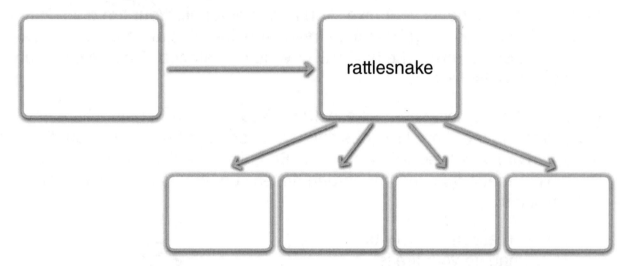

7. **Color in the most rattle segments a snake could have if it was three years old.**

Write two or more sentences that tell what each story is about.

8. **"To Hold or Not to Hold"** _____

_____

9. **"What Jillie Is Afraid Of"** _____

_____

10. **Why do you think a rattlesnake would want to warn you off rather than bite you?**

_____

_____

_____

What Leaks Out

Imagine you are riding your bike. You ride over a nail. Your tire goes flat. The nail has punctured the rubber tube inside the tire. The air in the tube has leaked out of the hole. The hole will have to be patched. The patched tube will have to be refilled with air.

Imagine you are riding your bike in 1840. You ride over a nail. The nail punctures the tire. Your tire goes flat, but air does not leak out! Your tire is not filled with air! It is filled with water. In 1840, tires were not made from rubber. They were made from leather garden hoses. Leather is a material made from animal skins.

Imagine you are riding your bike in 1843. Imagine your tire is punctured. This time, nothing leaks out! This is because your tire is a leather tube. The tube is wrapped in a strip of canvas. Canvas is a strong, heavy cloth. The tube is not filled with air or water. It is filled with grass or horsehair.

Imagine you are riding your bike in 1845. This time, if you run over a nail, air will leak out! This is because air-filled bike tubes were invented in 1845.

56

Why the Tires Had Screws

Kareem was looking at his Uncle Joe's bike. "Uncle Joe," said Kareem, "There is something very wrong with your bike. The tires are very fat and thick. They are bumpy, too. Even more strange, they have screws in them!"

Uncle Joe laughed. He said, "That's because this is a mountain bike. Mountain bike tires are thicker and wider than regular street bike tires. They have deeper and bumpier treads than regular street bike tires. The deeper and bumpier treads give me more traction. My wheels slip less when I have more traction."

"Yes," said Kareem. "But that doesn't explain why your tires have screws in them!"

Uncle Joe said, "My mountain bike tires were altered. They were changed for a reason. They were altered so I would get even more traction."

"Why would you need even more traction?" asked Kareem.

"For racing down steep ski slopes," answered Uncle Joe. "When the screws puncture the snow, I get more traction. Sometimes I go 70 miles per hour (112 kph)! At that speed, I need all the traction I can get."

"Uncle Joe," said Kareem, "I think you should take me next time you go biking down a ski slope!"

Show What You Know

Answer the questions on "What Leaks Out" and "Why the Tires Had Screws."
You may look back at what you have read if you need to.

1. **When something is punctured**
   - (A) it is patched.
   - (B) it is air-filled.
   - (C) nothing leaks out.
   - (D) a hole is made in it.

2. **When something is altered**
   - (A) it is changed.
   - (B) it is more stable.
   - (C) it has more traction.
   - (D) it races down a ski slope.

3. **Both stories are about**
   - (A) bike tires.
   - (B) racing tires.
   - (C) leaking tires.
   - (D) mountain bike tires.

4. **A tire made from a leather garden hose most likely**
   - (A) is a tire for a mountain bike.
   - (B) does not have a lot of traction.
   - (C) is best for going down a ski slope.
   - (D) does not leak if it is filled with water.

5. **A mountain bike is more stable than a regular street bike because**
   - (A) its tires are thin.
   - (B) its tires are fatter.
   - (C) its tires are filled with air.
   - (D) its tires are filled with grass.

Show What You Know (cont.)

6. **Fill in the chart.**

Year tires made	Filled with
1840	

7. **Write what bike each tire is most likely used for:** *regular street, regular mountain, snow mountain*

A.

B.

C.

_____ _____ _____

Write two or more sentences that tell what each story is about.

8. **"What Leaks Out"** _____

_____

9. **"Why the Tires Had Screws"** _____

_____

10. **Do you think Uncle Joe's tires are less likely to go flat than tires made in the 1800s? Tell why or why not.**

_____

_____

_____

Natural Wonders

There are many natural wonders. These wonders are not man-made. They are part of the natural world. Some natural wonders are amazing. They are so amazing that it is hard to believe they are real.

One natural wonder is a tree. The tree is very old. It is the oldest living tree in the world. It is so old that people have a hard time believing the tree is real. The tree is older than you. It is older than everyone you know. How old is the tree? The tree is over 4,725 years old! The tree is a type of pine tree. It grows in California.

Another natural wonder is a snake. The snake is very long. It is the longest snake in the world. The snake is so long that people have a hard time believing the snake is real. The snake is longer than you. It is longer than everyone you know. How long does the snake grow? It can grow up to 33 feet (10 m) long. How much can the snake weigh? It can weigh up to 300 pounds (135 kg). The snake is a type of python. It lives in Asia.

The Biggest Liar

Alejandro and Dana were having a contest. They were seeing who could tell the biggest lie. Yolanda was the judge. Yolanda would judge the lies. She would say who told the biggest lie.

Alejandro said, "When I was walking to school, I saw something big. It was large. It was enormous. It was a mouse as big as a horse!"

Dana said, "I didn't see a mouse as big as a horse. Maybe that mouse got eaten by the dog I saw. The dog was big. It was large. It was enormous. It was as big as a bus!"

Alejandro said, "I didn't see a dog as big as a bus. Maybe that dog got eaten by the spider I saw. The spider was big. It was large. It was enormous. It was as big as an airplane!"

Dana said, "I didn't see a spider as big as an airplane. Maybe that spider got eaten by the dinosaur I saw. The dinosaur was big. It was large. It was enormous. It was as big as a rocket ship!"

All of a sudden Yolanda stood up. Yolanda said, "I believe you both. When are you going to start telling lies so I can say who is the biggest liar?"

Show What You Know

Answer the questions on "Natural Wonders" and "The Biggest Liar."
You may look back at what you have read if you need to.

1. **The oldest tree is a type of**
   - (A) oak tree.
   - (B) pine tree.
   - (C) python tree.
   - (D) redwood tree.

2. **The spider was as big as**
   - (A) a bus.
   - (B) a horse.
   - (C) a dinosaur.
   - (D) an airplane.

3. **Both stories are about**
   - (A) amazing lies.
   - (B) natural wonders people can see.
   - (C) judging what lies are natural wonders.
   - (D) hard to believe natural wonders and lies.

4. **A fact is true. A fact is not made-up. A fact is real. What answer is a true fact and not just part of a story?**
   - (A) Dana saw a dog as big as a bus.
   - (B) A spider was as big as an airplane.
   - (C) The oldest tree grows in California.
   - (D) The longest snake is as big as a rocket ship.

5. **What thing from "The Biggest Liar" is not part of the natural world?**
   - (A) a bus
   - (B) a horse
   - (C) a snake
   - (D) a mouse

Show What You Know (cont.)

6. Fill in the information. Put an X in the box if the information is not in the story.

	oldest tree	longest snake
type		
how old		
how long		
where lives		

7. Complete the chart.

who said		Dana		
animal seen	mouse			dinosaur
as big as a			airplane	

Write two or more sentences that tell what each story is about.

8. "Natural Wonders" _____

_____

9. "The Biggest Liar" _____

_____

10. Think of an amazing natural wonder. Tell why you know it is real and not a lie.

_____

_____

Around the World in a Balloon

No one had ever done it. Many people had tried. Everyone had failed. Bertrand Piccard had tried before. He had tried two times. What had he tried to do and failed? He had tried to sail around the world in a hot air balloon without stopping.

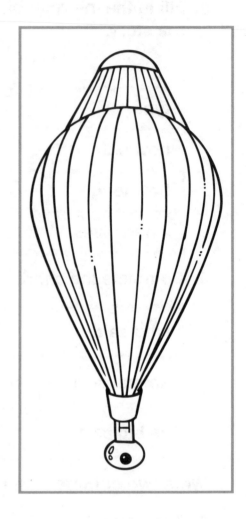

Now, Piccard was trying for a third time. He was scared. He threw up because he was so scared. Still, Piccard would not quit. On March 1, 1999, Piccard and his partner lifted off. Their balloon was 18 stories high. Piccard and his partner rode below the big balloon in a tiny capsule. The capsule was sealed, or closed.

The balloon went so high that ice formed on it. Over 300 pounds (135 kg) of ice formed on the balloon! Piccard and his partner had to quickly go lower. They had to get the heavy ice off, fast. Piccard climbed out of the capsule's hatch, or door. Using a fire ax, he knocked off the ice.

Piccard and his partner flew without stopping. After 19 days, 21 hours, and 55 minutes, they landed. They had not failed. They had gone around the world!

64

Aesop's Fable of the Thirsty Crow

Aesop was a storyteller. He lived a long time ago in Greece. All of Aesop's stories had a moral. A moral is a lesson. One of Aesop's stories was about a crow. The story goes like this:

A crow was very thirsty. The crow was so thirsty that it felt half dead. "I need water," the crow said. "I need water soon or I will die of thirst." Just then the crow came upon a pitcher. There was a little bit of water in the pitcher. The crow put his beak into the pitcher's mouth, but he could not drink the water. He could not reach it. The water level was too low.

The crow tried to reach the water again and again. He could not. The water level was too low. Then the crow thought of something. The crow found a tiny pebble. He picked up the pebble. He dropped it into the pitcher. Over and over the crow picked up tiny pebbles. Over and over he dropped the pebbles into the pitcher. Slowly, slowly, the level of the water rose. Finally, the water level was high enough for the crow to drink!

What is the moral of this fable? The moral is "little by little does the trick."

Show What You Know

Answer the questions on "Around the World in a Balloon" and "Aesop's Fable of the Thirsty Crow." You may look back at what you have read if you need to.

1. **How many stories high was Piccard's balloon?**
   - Ⓐ 18
   - Ⓑ 21
   - Ⓒ 55
   - Ⓓ 300

2. **Why couldn't the crow drink the water in the pitcher when it first tried?**
   - Ⓐ The water level was too low.
   - Ⓑ The water level was too high.
   - Ⓒ There were too many pebbles in the pitcher.
   - Ⓓ The crow could not put his beak into the pitcher's mouth.

3. **Both stories are about**
   - Ⓐ filling a tiny capsule.
   - Ⓑ going around the world.
   - Ⓒ being scared when one is thirsty.
   - Ⓓ trying over when the first time doesn't work.

4. **Piccard was like the thirsty crow because**
   - Ⓐ he was scared.
   - Ⓑ he sailed slowly.
   - Ⓒ he did not give up.
   - Ⓓ he filled a balloon.

5. **The crow could fill the pitcher with pebbles because**
   - Ⓐ the pitcher was sealed.
   - Ⓑ the crow used a fire ax.
   - Ⓒ the capsule was below the pitcher.
   - Ⓓ the crow could pick up the pebbles in its beak.

Show What You Know (cont.)

6. **List in order what happens in the story. Use the numbers 1 to 5. Put 1 by what happened first. Put 5 by what happened last.**

   _____ Piccard knocked off ice.

   _____ Piccard threw up.

   _____ Piccard failed two times.

   _____ Piccard sailed around the world.

   _____ Piccard's balloon sailed very high.

7. **Circle the two pitchers that have the same amount of water.**

   A.   B.   C.

Write two or more sentences that tell what each story is about.

8. **"Around the World in a Balloon"** _____

   _____

9. **"Aesop's Fable of the Thirsty Crow"** _____

   _____

10. **It took Piccard three tries to sail around the world. Think of something you learned to do. It might be riding a bike, tying your shoe, swimming, reading, or skating. You pick! Then, tell how you learned. Did it take three times? Was it "little by little" or all at once?**

    _____

    _____

    _____

Animals with Closed Nostrils

You have a nose. Your nose has two nostrils. Air goes in and out of your nose through your nostrils. Your nostrils are always open. They do not close.

Sea lions and seals, on the other hand, have two nostrils that are normally closed! If a sea lion or seal wants to breathe, it has to use a special muscle. The special muscle opens the nostrils. It opens the nostrils so the animal can breathe. When the animal relaxes the muscles, the nostrils close. They snap shut.

You breathe air. Sea lions and seals breathe air. So why do sea lions and seals have nostrils that are normally closed? Sea lions and seals spend a lot of time under the water. They need to keep their nostrils closed to keep the water out. They only open their nostrils when their heads are out of the water and they need to breathe.

Sea lions look like seals, but they are different. Sea lions have ears. True seals do not have ears. Sea lions use their front flippers to push them through the water. They use their rear flippers to steer. Seals use their front flippers to steer. They use their rear flippers to push them through the water.

Getting What Kate Wanted

Kate said, "Dad, you can't get me what I want for my birthday. I want to see a lion free in the wild. I want to get so close to a wild lion that I can hear it roar. You can't get me what I want."

On Kate's birthday, Kate's dad took Kate to a cave on the Oregon coast. To get to the cave, Kate and her dad rode in an elevator. The elevator went over 200 feet (60 m) down. When they stepped out of the elevator into the dim cave, Kate's dad led Kate to a chain link fence. Kate saw large animals on the other side of the chain link fence. Some of the animals were lying on rocks. Others were leaping in and out of the ocean.

Kate's dad said, "You are looking at wild lions, Kate! What type of lions are they? They are sea lions! See the one with the mane? That is a bull, or male sea lion." As Kate looked, the bull raised its head. It roared! Its roar echoed through the cave.

Kate laughed. She said, "Dad, you did get me what I asked for. You just did it with a different kind of lion than I was expecting!"

Show What You Know

Answer the questions on "Animals with Closed Nostrils" and "Getting What Kate Wanted." You may look back at what you have read if you need to.

1. **Sea lions and seals have closed nostrils because**
   - (A) they breathe air.
   - (B) they are animals with noses.
   - (C) they spend a lot of time under the water.
   - (D) they use a special muscle to relax their nostrils.

2. **You can tell that Kate saw wild sea lions because**
   - (A) the sea lions were lying on rocks.
   - (B) the bull raised its head and roared.
   - (C) the sea lions were on the other side of the fence.
   - (D) the sea lions were leaping in and out of the ocean.

3. **What did both of these stories have in common?**
   - (A) seals
   - (B) two kinds of lions
   - (C) seeing sea lions in a cave
   - (D) an animal whose nostrils snap shut

4. **Pick the answer that makes this sentence true: If a sea lion is relaxing all of its muscles,**
   - (A) it is not a bull.
   - (B) it is not roaring.
   - (C) it is not breathing air.
   - (D) it is not under the water.

5. **Kate did not think she would get what she wanted for her birthday because she**
   - (A) did not know about sea lions.
   - (B) did not know male sea lions were called bulls.
   - (C) did not know seals and sea lions were different.
   - (D) did not know she was going to ride in an elevator.

Show What You Know (cont.)

6. **Fill in the chart.**

	sea lions	seals
ears		
front flippers used for		
back flippers used for		

7. **Fill in the blanks.**

   What did Kate want? _____

   Where did Kate go? _____

   When did Kate go? _____

   Why did Kate go? _____

   How did Kate go? _____

Write two or more sentences that tell what each story is about.

8. **"Animals with Closed Nostrils"** _____

   _____

9. **"Getting What Kate Wanted"** _____

   _____

10. **Think about the cave Kate when into. It was dim. A chain link fence went across part of it. Tell why you think the cave was dim and had a chain link fence.**

   _____

   _____

   _____

Grass Trimmers and Spies

Woodrow Wilson was President of the United States. He was President from 1913 to 1921. He was the 28th President. Wilson was President at a time of war. He was President during World War I. People needed to save money during the war. They needed to use less.

Wilson thought of a way to save money. He thought of a way to use less. He had a flock of sheep brought to the White House. The sheep ate the grass on the White House lawn. The sheep got free food. The White House got its lawn trimmed. There was only one problem. The hungry sheep ate more than the grass! They ate all of the White House flowers, too!

People in the White House were pleased about the sheep. They were not pleased about something else. They were not pleased about a tapping noise. People were afraid the noise came from spies. They were afraid spies were tapping out secret messages about the war.

People were no longer afraid when they found out who was making the tapping noise. It was not a spy who was tapping. It was a bird! It was a woodpecker! The woodpecker was tapping on the White House's copper gutters.

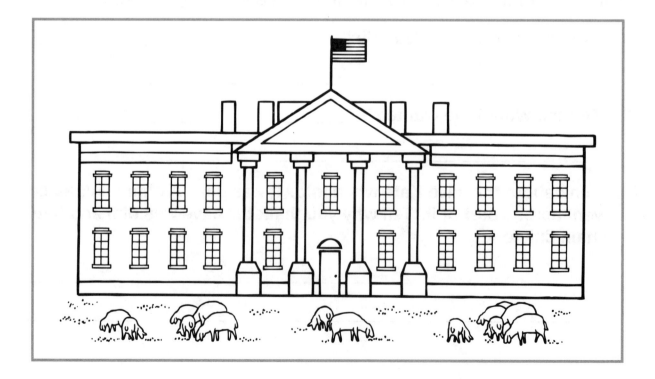

Carol and the Spies

Carol said, "Mom, I'll get the lawn mowed. I won't forget."

Carol's mom smiled. She said, "No, I don't think you will."

Carol put on her sweatshirt. She walked to the park. On the way, a lady walking her dog asked, "Is the mowing done?" Carol was startled. How did the lady know she should mow the lawn?

When Carol got to the park, a boy said, "Is the lawn mowing done?" Carol was startled. How did the boy know she was supposed to mow the lawn? After several more people asked Carol about the mowing, she began to get scared. How did people know she needed to mow the lawn? Was she being followed by spies?

Puzzled, Carol left the park. She went home and got the lawn mowed. She went to tell her friend Suzu about the spies. As she went in the door to Suzu's house, Suzu's father walked out. "I hope you finished mowing the lawn," he said.

When Carol nodded yes, Suzu's father said, "Then I'll take this off." He removed a paper that Carol's mother had taped to the back of Carol's sweatshirt. A message was written on the paper. What did the message say? It said, "Please remind me to mow the lawn."

Show What You Know

Answer the questions on "Grass Trimmers and Spies" and "Carol and the Spies."
You may look back at what you have read if you need to.

1. **What is not true of Woodrow Wilson?**
   - Ⓐ He was the 28th President.
   - Ⓑ He was afraid of spending less.
   - Ⓒ He was President from 1913 to 1921.
   - Ⓓ He was President during World War I.

2. **When Carol was startled she was**
   - Ⓐ suddenly finished.
   - Ⓑ suddenly followed.
   - Ⓒ suddenly reminded.
   - Ⓓ suddenly surprised.

3. **What do both stories have in common?**
   - Ⓐ birds
   - Ⓑ sheep
   - Ⓒ mowing
   - Ⓓ Presidents

4. **What is true about the spies?**
   - Ⓐ They were real in both of the stories.
   - Ⓑ They were real in only one of the stories.
   - Ⓒ They were not real in both of the stories.
   - Ⓓ They were not real in only one of the stories.

5. **Carol thought she was being spied upon because she did not know**
   - Ⓐ what her mom had done.
   - Ⓑ that it was a time of war.
   - Ⓒ what was making the tapping noise.
   - Ⓓ that her mother had thought of a way to spend less.

Show What You Know (cont.)

6. **Fill in the boxes. What people . . .**

   wanted the sheep to do

   did not want the sheep to do

7. **Make a list of all the people who talked to Carol. List them in the order they spoke in the story.**

   1. _____

   2. _____

   3. _____

   4. several more people at park

   5. _____

Write two or more sentences that tell what each story is about.

8. **"Grass Trimmers and Spies"** _____

   _____

9. **"Carol and the Spies"** _____

   _____

10. **It does not say in the story how Carol got the lawn mowed. Do you think she got her lawn trimmed the same way President Wilson did? Tell why or why not.**

    _____

    _____

    _____

Spitting Crickets

Every year in West Lafayette, Indiana, there is a contest. Some people think the contest is strange. Other people think the contest is gross and yucky. What is the contest about? It is about spitting crickets! The crickets are real. They are not plastic. They are not rubber.

The contest is to see who can spit a dead cricket the farthest. The crickets are all about the same size. They are freeze-dried. Then they are thawed for the contest. Contestants pick a cricket from a tray. The cricket must be fully intact. It cannot be missing any parts. Contestants must put the cricket all the way in their mouths. They must spit it out within 20 seconds.

When the cricket lands, it is checked. It is checked for six legs. It is checked for four wings. It is checked for two antennas. If the cricket is intact, the "spit" counts. The distance the cricket was spat is measured. The winner is the person who spat the cricket the farthest.

How far can people spit crickets? Some people have spit crickets over 32 feet (9.6 m)! Is there a trick to winning? Some contestants say to put the cricket far back in one's mouth. They say the cricket's head should face forward.

The Rich Man's Contest

A rich man held a contest. The rich man said, "The contest is to try and fill this room. The person who fills this room the most will win. The winner will get half of my money. You can fill this room with anything you want, but you must be able to carry it yourself."

Three people entered the contest. Each person went to town. The first person came back with a big sack of feathers. It was so heavy he could barely carry it. The first person spread the feathers all around. The feathers covered one corner of the room.

The second person came back with an even bigger sack of straw. It was so heavy he could barely carry it. The second person spread the straw all around. The straw covered two corners of the room.

The third person came back. It looked like he wasn't carrying anything. He walked into the room. Everybody began to laugh. No one thought he could win. Then the third person reached into his pocket. He pulled out a candle and a book of matches. He lit the candle. Its light filled the entire room. The third person had carried the least, but he had won.

Show What You Know

Answer the questions on "Spitting Crickets" and "The Rich Man's Contest."
You may look back at what you have read if you need to.

1. **If something is intact, it**
   (A) is not thawed.
   (B) is not plastic.
   (C) is not gross or yucky.
   (D) is not missing any parts.

2. **The rich man's contest was**
   (A) to carry the most.
   (B) to spread straw the most.
   (C) to spit crickets the most.
   (D) to fill the room the most.

3. **What do both stories have in common?**
   (A) They both are about contests.
   (B) They both are about what to do.
   (C) They both are about people who win.
   (D) They both are about spreading things.

4. **A contestant in a cricket spitting contest must**
   (A) freeze-dry his or her own cricket.
   (B) fit his or her cricket in a pocket.
   (C) spit out his or her cricket within 20 seconds.
   (D) try to spit the cricket into the farthest corner.

5. **In "The Rich Man's Contest," you can tell that the people who laughed**
   (A) did not know what the man had in his pocket.
   (B) did not know the candle had been freeze-dried.
   (C) did not know about the sack in the man's mouth.
   (D) did not know about the book of matches on the tray.

Show What You Know (cont.)

6. **Fill in the chart to show what the crickets were checked for.**

Part	Legs		
Number		4	

7. **Fill in the chart to show who brought what.**

	what carried	space filled
Person 1		
Person 2		
Person 3		

Write two or more sentences that tell what each story is about.

8. **"Spitting Crickets"** _____

_____

9. **"The Rich Man's Contest"** _____

_____

10. **Think about the contests in the stories. Both contests had rules. Do you think the rules helped to make the contests fair? Tell why or why not. Use an example from the stories in your answer.**

_____

_____

_____

Dallas and the Bull

Dallas was a farmer. He lived in Indiana. Dallas grew corn and soybeans on his farm. He also raised cattle. One time, a baby calf lost its mother. Dallas had to take care of the calf. Dallas fed the calf several times each day. He used a baby bottle made for calves. The calf was very smart. It learned to recognize Dallas. The calf would wait for Dallas. When it saw Dallas, the calf would come running.

The calf grew quickly. Soon, it did not need a bottle. It grew into an enormous bull. The bull was grown-up, but it still recognized Dallas. Whenever the bull saw Dallas, it would run over to the fence. It would wait for Dallas to give him a treat.

One day, the ground was very muddy. It was very slippery. Dallas was working by the pasture. Across the pasture, the bull recognized his friend. The bull started to run to Dallas as fast as it could. It ran so fast that it slipped on the muddy ground! His back legs slipped under him. The bull was sitting down, but he did not stop coming! Dallas had to jump to safety as the surprised bull slid across the muddy pasture and right through the fence!

An American Folktale: The Great Blue Ox

Paul Bunyan was a giant lumberjack. He cut down trees in Minnesota. One winter, it was so cold that the snow turned blue. Paul was walking through the blue snow when he found a teeny-tiny baby ox. Paul took the wet, cold ox back to his fire. The blue snow had stained the ox so Paul named him Babe the Blue Ox.

Babe was a fast growing calf. He grew so fast that folks who stared at him for five minutes could see him grow. He grew so big that 42 ax handles could fit between his eyes. He grew so big that it took a crow a whole day to fly from one horn to the other.

Babe would pull anything with two ends. Paul gave Babe the end of twisty roads. Babe would pull the roads straight. One day, Babe pulled so many roads straight that there were 20 miles (32 km) of left over roads with nowhere to go. Paul just rolled up the extra roads and used them to lay a new road into new timberland.

Minnesota has 10,000 lakes. Where did these lakes come from? They are footprints. They are the left behind footprints of Paul Bunyan and Babe the Blue Ox.

Show What You Know

Answer the questions on "Dallas and the Bull" and "An American Folktale: The Great Blue Ox." You may look back at what you have read if you need to.

1. **What is not true about Dallas?**
   Ⓐ Dallas grew soybeans.
   Ⓑ Dallas lived in Indiana.
   Ⓒ Dallas was a lumberjack.
   Ⓓ Dallas gave treats to his bull.

2. **How long did people have to stare at Babe to see him grow?**
   Ⓐ 1 minute
   Ⓑ 5 minutes
   Ⓒ 42 minutes
   Ⓓ 10,000 minutes

3. **What do both stories have in common?**
   Ⓐ men who raised baby calves
   Ⓑ men who straightened fences
   Ⓒ men who farmed and raised cattle
   Ⓓ men who worked where it was very snowy

4. **The bull slid right through the fence because**
   Ⓐ it wanted a treat.
   Ⓑ it recognized his friend Dallas.
   Ⓒ it had slipped on the muddy ground.
   Ⓓ it was pulling on the roads to make them straight.

5. **What did Paul do with the extra roads?**
   Ⓐ He used them to make a pasture.
   Ⓑ He used them to lay a new road.
   Ⓒ He used them to stain Babe blue.
   Ⓓ He used them to go from one of Babe's horns to the other.

82

Show What You Know (cont.)

6. **Look at each pair of sentences. Write "before" or "after" on each line.**

_____ Dallas fed the calf.	_____ The bull slipped.
_____ The calf recognized Dallas.	_____ The pasture was muddy.

7. **The story about Babe is fiction. It is not real. Write down four things about Babe that make you know the story is fiction.**

   1. _____

   2. _____

   3. _____

   4. _____

Write two or more sentences that tell what each story is about.

8. **"Dallas and the Bull"** _____

   _____

9. **"An American Folktale: The Great Blue Ox"** _____

   _____

10. **Babe made lakes with his footprints. If Dallas's bull was in a folktale, what might his bull have made when he slid across the pasture and through the fence?**

   _____

   _____

   _____

Champion on Ice

Sasha Cohen is a champion on ice. She is a figure skater. A figure skater is an athlete. A figure skater skates, dances, and jumps on the ice. No one becomes a champion over night. One must work hard. One must practice many hours. Sasha worked hard to become a champion figure skater.

Sasha had to learn to jump on the ice. She had to learn to turn in the air while she was jumping. When Sasha was learning, she fell many times. She had lots of bruises. She was black and blue all over. Then Sasha saw another girl skating who was wearing a pair of padded shorts. Sasha thought the padded shorts were a great idea. As fast as she could, she got some for herself!

Sasha learned her jumps in steps. At first, she would land on two feet after turning. This would help lessen the falling. This would help keep the number of bruises down. Then she would practice landing on one foot. One time, Sasha had to practice one kind of jump many times. While practicing, Sasha's left skate blade hit the tip of her right boot many times. Sasha hit it so many times that she sliced the toe of the boot right off!

Practicing with the Speed Team

Ryan was excited. The speed skating race would soon start. Ryan was going to skate in the race. Ryan knew he wouldn't win. He just wanted to be noticed so he would be asked to join the Speed Team. Ryan knew that if he practiced with the Speed Team he would become a faster, better ice skater.

As Ryan was lacing his skates, he noticed another ice skater on the bench next to him. The other skater's name was Claus. Claus was the fastest skater on the Speed Team. Ryan noticed that Claus didn't look happy. He asked Claus what was wrong.

Claus held up a broken lace. He said, "My lace is broken. I cannot skate. Don't worry about me. Hurry! Get on the ice so you don't miss the race."

Quietly, Ryan removed the lace from his own skate. He handed it to Claus. Claus was very surprised. Ryan said, "You have to skate. Your team is depending on you. I will race you another time."

With Ryan's lace, Claus easily won the race. Then, after the race, something very exciting happened. Claus invited Ryan to practice with the Speed Team! "You're going to need lots of practice," said Claus grinning, "if you ever expect to beat me!"

Show What You Know

Answer the questions on "Champion on Ice" and "Practicing with the Speed Team." You may look back at what you have read if you need to.

1. When Sasha jumps, she tries to
- (A) turn in the air.
- (B) slice her boot toe off.
- (C) always land on two feet.
- (D) become a champion over night.

2. Ryan wanted to practice with the Speed Team so
- (A) he could skate in a race.
- (B) he could become a champion.
- (C) he could become a faster ice skater.
- (D) he could learn how to jump on the ice.

3. Both stories are about
- (A) ice skating.
- (B) speed skating.
- (C) figure skating.
- (D) champion skating.

4. You can tell that Sasha
- (A) never broke a lace.
- (B) didn't practice much.
- (C) liked getting bruises.
- (D) noticed other skaters.

5. You can tell that Claus
- (A) had practiced jumping many times.
- (B) thought Ryan would lend him a lace.
- (C) knew that champions were not made over night.
- (D) did not want Ryan to race in the speed skating race.

Show What You Know (cont.)

6. Use checks to show what Sasha might do if she is still learning a jump and what she would do if she has learned the jump.

What Sasha does	still learning	knows the jump
falls	✓	
turns in air		
slices boot toe		
lands on two feet		
lands on one foot		

7. Ryan noticed that Claus didn't look happy. Draw a picture of Claus' face to show what he looked like when Ryan noticed him.

Write two or more sentences that tell what each story is about.

8. "Champion on Ice" _____

_____

9. "Practicing with the Speed Team" _____

_____

10. Sasha wore padded shorts when she was first learning how to jump. What do you think a speed skater wears when he or she first practices skating fast? Tell why. Do you think they wear padded shorts? Tell why or why not.

_____

_____

_____

Skeleton Information

You have a skeleton. It is made of 206 bones. What does your skeleton do? Your skeleton protects important organs in your body. It holds you up. It helps you move. Muscles are attached to parts of your skeleton. Together, muscles and bones make your body move.

Some skeleton bones are big. Other bones are small. The biggest bone is the thigh bone in the leg. It is called the femur. The femur runs from the hip down to the knee. The smallest bone is in the ear. It is called the stirrup. It is about the size of a grain of rice.

What keeps your skeleton together? What attaches your muscles to your bones? Ligaments and tendons do. Ligaments and tendons are like tough bands. They are made of tough material. Ligaments hold the bones in place. They run from one bone to the next. They keep your bones from pulling or slipping apart.

Tendons are bands that connect muscles to bones. Your Achilles tendon is right behind your ankle. It connects your calf muscle to your heel bone. The Achilles tendon is the biggest tendon. It is the strongest tendon.

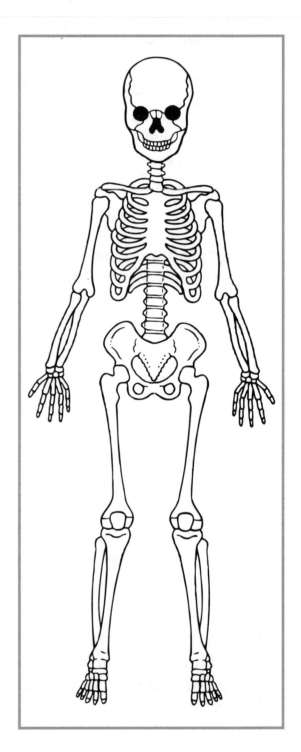

The Warrior with a Weak Spot

The Greeks had many myths. A myth is a story. One myth was about Achilles. Achilles was a great warrior. He fought in the Trojan War. He was the bravest warrior in the war. He was the handsomest warrior in the war. He was the greatest warrior in the war.

Arrows would not stop Achilles. Swords would not stop Achilles. Spears would not attack Achilles. This was because Achilles was protected. He was protected by something his mother had done. When Achilles was a baby, his mother had picked him up. She held him by one heel. She dipped him in the waters of the River Styx. The waters protected Achilles. They made him strong. They made it so nothing could hurt him.

Achilles had only one weak spot. His only weak spot was on his heel. It was where his mother had held him when she dipped him in the river. Achilles died when an arrow hit him. The arrow hit him in the heel. The arrow was shot by a man, but it was guided by Apollo. Apollo was a god in Greek myths. It was Apollo who guided the arrow to Achilles' only weak spot.

Show What You Know

Answer the questions on "Skeleton Information" and "The Warrior with a Weak Spot." You may look back at what you have read if you need to.

1. **A muscle is connected to a bone by**
   - Ⓐ a femur.
   - Ⓑ a tendon.
   - Ⓒ a stirrup.
   - Ⓓ a ligament.

2. **Achilles' one weak spot was on his**
   - Ⓐ heel.
   - Ⓑ foot.
   - Ⓒ hand.
   - Ⓓ face.

3. **What did you read about in both stories?**
   - Ⓐ arrow
   - Ⓑ Apollo
   - Ⓒ attach
   - Ⓓ Achilles

4. **A skeleton is like being dipped in the waters of the River Styx because a skeleton**
   - Ⓐ helps you move.
   - Ⓑ is held together by ligaments.
   - Ⓒ helps to protect important organs.
   - Ⓓ is made up of very big and very small bones.

5. **Most likely, Achilles would not have died if**
   - Ⓐ a god had not guided the arrow.
   - Ⓑ his muscles had not been attached.
   - Ⓒ he had not been such a great warrior.
   - Ⓓ his femur had not run down to his heel bone.

Show What You Know (cont.)

6. List three things your skeleton does.

1. _____

2. _____

3. _____

7. Fill in the boxes to show what happened in the story.

1. Achilles' mother holds Achilles by his heel.	2.	3. Achilles is protected except for one spot.

4. Achilles fights in the Trojan War.	5.

Write two or more sentences that tell what each story is about.

8. "Skeleton Information" _____

_____

9. "The Warrior with a Weak Spot" _____

_____

10. Do you think the Achilles tendon was named for the Achilles in the Greek myth? Tell why or why not.

_____

_____

_____

A Special Kind of Orphanage

An orphanage is a home. It is a place where orphans live. An orphan has lost its parents. There is a special orphanage in Kenya. Kenya is a country in Africa. The orphanage is not for people. It is for baby elephants.

Sometimes elephants are killed by poachers. Poachers break the law. They hunt where they are not allowed. Poachers kill adult elephants. They kill them for their tusks. The tusks are made out of ivory. The poachers sell the ivory tusks for money. The baby elephants are left all alone. They do not know how to take care of themselves.

People are working hard to stop poaching. They are working hard to help the elephant orphans, too. Baby elephants eat every few minutes. They drink milk. They drink milk until they are two. Then, they start eating grass. They do not stop drinking milk until they are five.

At the orphanage, workers work all day. They work all night. They feed the elephants every few minutes. Workers do not care for just one baby. They switch around. This is so the babies do not get too attached to one person. This is so one day the orphans can be set free. They can go back to the wild.

Hunting Elephants

Kim was hunting. She was hunting elephants. Kim was not hunting elephants with a gun. She was hunting elephants with a camera. Kim was in Kenya. She was on safari. A safari is a journey or a hunting trip.

Kim had a guide. The guide said, "You must stay in the jeep. You must not get out. The elephants you see are wild. They do not know you only have a camera."

Kim took many pictures. She liked seeing the elephants bathing in the water. She liked it when the elephants sprayed themselves with water. Kim's guide said, "See how they pick up water? They use their trunks. A trunk is an elephant's nose. Elephants have the longest noses. No other living animal has a longer nose."

Just then, Kim saw some other elephants. Some were rolling in the mud. Others were spraying themselves. They were using their trunks to spray dust. Kim's guide said, "Elephants don't just take water baths. They take mud baths. They take dust showers. The mud and dust dries on their skin. It makes a kind of armor. What is this armor for? What does this dirt armor protect them from? It protects the big elephants from tiny insect bites!"

Show What You Know

Answer the questions on "A Special Kind of Orphanage" and "Hunting Elephants." You may look back at what you have read if you need to.

1. **How old are elephants when they stop drinking milk?**
   Ⓐ one
   Ⓑ two
   Ⓒ four
   Ⓓ five

2. **You are most likely on safari if you**
   Ⓐ are walking through a zoo.
   Ⓑ are riding your bike to school.
   Ⓒ are driving in a fast-moving car.
   Ⓓ are taking pictures of animals in the wild.

3. **What do both stories have in common?**
   Ⓐ They both are about poaching elephants.
   Ⓑ They both are about what elephants eat.
   Ⓒ They both are about animals with long noses.
   Ⓓ They both are about going on safari in Kenya.

4. **Most likely, baby elephants**
   Ⓐ do not have tusks.
   Ⓑ do not have trunks.
   Ⓒ do not take mud baths.
   Ⓓ do not take dust showers.

5. **Elephants roll in the mud to**
   Ⓐ protect themselves from hunters.
   Ⓑ protect themselves from poachers.
   Ⓒ protect themselves from insect bites.
   Ⓓ protect themselves from people on safari.

Show What You Know (cont.)

6. **Fill in the blanks.**

   What are orphanages? _____

   Where is the orphanage in the story? _____

   When are elephants taken to the orphanage?_____

   Why are elephants shot by poachers? _____

   How do workers keep elephants from becoming too attached?_____

   _____

7. **There are four paragraphs in the story "Hunting Elephants." Fill in the boxes. Each box should tell the big idea of one paragraph.**

Paragraph 1	Paragraph 2	Paragraph 3	Paragraph 4
	Kim's guide tells her the elephants are wild.		

Write two or more sentences that tell what each story is about.

8. **"A Special Kind of Orphanage"** _____

   _____

9. **"Hunting Elephants"** _____

   _____

10. **How is hunting with a camera different than poaching? How are they the same?**

    _____

    _____

    _____

A Different Kind of Lesson

Tiger Woods' father cheated. He cheated on purpose! Tiger was a young boy. He played golf. Tiger's father was a grown man. Still, Tiger's father cheated. He cheated in many different ways. One way was with noise. Tiger's father would wait until Tiger was about to swing his golf club. Then, just as Tiger was about to swing, Tiger's father might cough. He might jingle coins. He might rip open his golf glove.

Other times, Tiger's father cheated by moving. He would wait until Tiger was about to putt. He would wait where Tiger could see him. Then, just as Tiger was about to putt, Tiger's father would move. He might sit. He might stand. He might turn. He might bend. He might wave. He broke the rules by moving.

Why did Tiger's father cheat? Tiger's father wanted to give Tiger a lesson. It was not a golf lesson. It was a different kind of lesson. It was a lesson on paying attention. Tiger's father did not want Tiger to pay attention to noise. He did not want Tiger to pay attention to movement. He wanted Tiger to only think about the game. He wanted Tiger to think about nothing else.

Why Tim Didn't Pay Attention

Ms. Sanchez was telling the class a story about golf. She was telling them about a king who banned golf. "The king was King James II," Ms. Sanchez said. "King James was an English king. He banned golf in 1457. He made it against the law to play. Why . . ."

Ms. Sanchez could not finish her sentence. Tim interrupted her. "Ms. Sanchez!" cried Tim. "There is a zebra in the school yard!"

Ms. Sanchez said gently, "Tim, you cannot interrupt me. It is rude. Please listen to me. Please pay attention." Then Ms. Sanchez went on with her lesson. "Why was golf banned? The king felt …"

Once again Tim interrupted. "Ms. Sanchez," he cried, "There really is a zebra!"

Ms. Sanchez shook her head in anger. She said, "You must not interrupt. You must pay attention. When I am done talking, you can raise your hand. Then you can talk." Ms. Sanchez continued with the lesson. "The king banned golf because he felt people were spending too much time playing. He did not want them to practice golf. He wanted them to practice shooting arrows."

Just then, another teacher came rushing in. She said, "Look out the window! You can see a zebra! The zebra escaped from the zoo!"

Show What You Know

Answer the questions on "A Different Kind of Lesson" and "Why Tim Didn't Pay Attention." You may look back at what you have read if you need to.

1. **What might Tiger Woods' father do just as Tiger was about to putt?**
   - Ⓐ He might wave.
   - Ⓑ He might cough.
   - Ⓒ He might jingle coins.
   - Ⓓ He might rip open his golf glove.

2. **The king banned golf because he wanted people to**
   - Ⓐ practice playing golf.
   - Ⓑ practice shooting arrows.
   - Ⓒ practice paying attention.
   - Ⓓ practice thinking about the game.

3. **Both stories are about**
   - Ⓐ cheating on purpose.
   - Ⓑ when to pay attention.
   - Ⓒ interrupting golf players.
   - Ⓓ banning zebras from playing golf.

4. **Most likely, if someone told Tiger Woods a zebra was close by, Tiger would not pay attention**
   - Ⓐ if he wanted to cheat.
   - Ⓑ if he wanted golf banned.
   - Ⓒ if he was about to swing.
   - Ⓓ if he was looking out a window.

5. **Most likely, Ms. Sanchez would not have minded Tim interrupting her if**
   - Ⓐ Tim had talked about King James II.
   - Ⓑ the other teacher had made more noise.
   - Ⓒ Tiger's father had taught her to pay attention.
   - Ⓓ she had known a zebra had escaped from the zoo.

Show What You Know (cont.)

6. Tiger's father did things so Tiger would not pay attention to noise or movement. Fill in the boxes to show what he did.

Noise

Movement

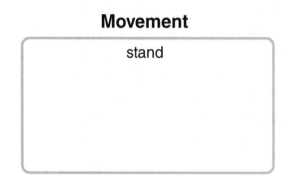

stand

7. Follow the talking! List in order the people who talked in the story "Why Tim Didn't Pay Attention."

1st _____   4th _____

2nd _____   5th _____

3rd _____Ms. Sanchez_____   6th _____

Write two or more sentences that tell what each story is about.

8. "A Different Kind of Lesson" _____

_____

9. "Why Tim Didn't Pay Attention" _____

_____

10. If Tim were watching Tiger Woods, do you think Tim would interrupt Tiger? Tell why or why not.

_____

_____

_____

What Cowboys Use

Ask a person how a cowboy gets around. Most people answer "horse." They do not answer "helicopter." There is a place where the answer is not "horse." It is "helicopter"! The place is Australia. Australia is a country. It's a continent too. It's the smallest continent.

In Australia, ranches are called stations. Some stations are big. It takes three or four days to travel across them. Cattle are raised on the stations. Sheep are too. The animals roam. They roam far and wide. They go all over the station. They eat dry grass. They drink water drawn from wells.

Jackaroos are boy ranch hands. Jillaroos are girl ranch hands. Jackaroos and jillaroos round up cattle and sheep. They travel far. They travel all over the station. They find the animals. They herd the animals back to the station. The distance is great. It is too far to walk. It is too far for a horse.

What do the jackaroos and jillaroos do? They use helicopters! They use motor bikes too. Helicopters are used to find the animals. They are used to herd the animals. Closer to the station, ranch hands are on motor bikes. They use their motor bikes to herd the animals. They herd the animals into large pens.

What Side to Walk On

Bessie and Mato were walking. They were walking along the road. Bessie said, "There is not a sidewalk so we are walking on the road. We are being careful. We are walking on the left-hand side of the road. This is because we are pedestrians. Pedestrians are walkers. Pedestrians are not drivers. Drivers drive on the right-hand side of the road. Pedestrians are supposed to walk against car traffic."

Mato and Bessie were riding bikes. They were riding bikes along the road. Mato said, "There is not a sidewalk so we are riding on the road. We are being careful. We are riding on the right-hand side of the road. This is because bikes are supposed to go in the same direction as cars."

Bessie and Mato knew the rules. They knew what side of the road to walk on. They knew what side of the road to ride bikes on. Then Bessie and Mato left home. They left the United States. They went to Australia. In Australia, the rules changed! Pedestrians walked on the right. Bike riders rode on the left. Why did the rules change? In Australia, drivers do not drive on the right-hand side of the road! They drive on the left.

Show What You Know

Answer the questions on "What Cowboys Use" and "What Side to Walk On."
You may look back at what you have read if you need to.

1. **Motor bikes are used to herd the animals**
   - Ⓐ into pens.
   - Ⓑ far and wide.
   - Ⓒ back into the station.
   - Ⓓ that are very far away.

2. **When there is not a sidewalk, pedestrians are supposed to walk**
   - Ⓐ against car traffic.
   - Ⓑ in the same direction as car traffic.
   - Ⓒ in the same direction as bike traffic.
   - Ⓓ on the same side in the United States and Australia.

3. **What are both stories about?**
   - Ⓐ Bessie the jillaroo and Mato the jackaroo
   - Ⓑ the way some things are done in Australia
   - Ⓒ the direction cattle and sheep should roam
   - Ⓓ how pedestrians ride in helicopters and on motor bikes

4. **If a cowboy uses a helicopter, most likely the cowboy is working on a**
   - Ⓐ small bike.
   - Ⓑ small ranch.
   - Ⓒ large station.
   - Ⓓ large continent.

5. **From the stories, you can tell that**
   - Ⓐ Australia is a small country.
   - Ⓑ not every country has the same rules.
   - Ⓒ not every country has sheep and cattle.
   - Ⓓ Australia is a bigger country than the United States.

Show What You Know (cont.)

6. Fill in the chart.

Word used in the

United States	Australia
ranch	
	jillaroo
boy ranch hand	

7. Draw a road. Draw cars and pedestrians on the road. Draw arrows to show what direction the cars and pedestrians are going. Write "United States" or "Australia" to show what country your road is in.

Write two or more sentences that tell what each story is about.

8. "What Cowboys Use" _____

   _____

9. "What Side to Walk On" _____

   _____

10. Why do you think pedestrians are supposed to walk against car and bike traffic?

   _____

   _____

   _____

The Elephant that Made a Word

Jumbo means large. It means bigger than usual. If something is jumbo sized, it is extra large. It is very big. It is huge. It is giant. An elephant helped make the word "jumbo." How can this be?

P.T. Barnum owned a circus. In 1881, Barnum bought an elephant. He bought it from a zoo. The elephant's name was Jumbo. Barnum bought Jumbo for his circus. Jumbo was very big. He was huge. He was giant. He was one of the largest elephants ever seen.

Everyone wanted to see Jumbo. They wanted to see how big he was. "He's so big!" they all said. "He's huge! He's giant! He's the biggest animal in the world!" Everyone talked about Jumbo. He became famous. Everyone knew who Jumbo was. His size had made him famous.

Pretty soon, people began to use Jumbo's name. They used it to mean something big. Instead of saying something was big, people would say it was "Jumbo." They meant it was big like Jumbo the elephant. So many people used Jumbo's name to mean big that it became a new word! Today, jumbo is a real word. It is a word that means big.

The Easel Guess

Ms. Ta said, "Students, I want you to guess. I want you to guess how the word 'easel' came about. An easel is a standing frame. Artists use easels. They use them when they paint their pictures. They use easels to hold up their pictures when they paint. Guess how this word came about."

The students guessed that the word "easel" came from the word "easy." They guessed this because they said using an easel makes it easier to paint.

Ms. Ta said, "Class, that was an excellent guess, but the word comes from the name of an animal! It comes from the word 'donkey'!"

Ms. Ta smiled at her students. She said, "You look puzzled. Let me explain. 'Ezel' is the Dutch word for donkey. In the 1600s, Dutch painters called their standing frames 'ezels.' They did this for two reasons. First, they thought the frames looked somewhat like a donkey. Second, the frames carried a burden. A burden is anything that is carried. It is a load. The frames carried their pictures in the same way a donkey carries burdens or loads.

"The use of the word 'ezel' spread. Pretty soon English painters used it too. Over time the English spelling became 'easel.'"

Show What You Know

Answer the questions on "The Elephant that Made a Word" and "The Easel Guess." You may look back at what you have read if you need to.

1. **What made Jumbo so famous?**
   - Ⓐ his name
   - Ⓑ his size
   - Ⓒ his owner
   - Ⓓ his circus

2. **The word "easel" comes from**
   - Ⓐ an elephant.
   - Ⓑ a Dutch word.
   - Ⓒ the word "essay."
   - Ⓓ an English word.

3. **What do both stories have in common?**
   - Ⓐ They are both about new words.
   - Ⓑ They are both about Dutch words.
   - Ⓒ They are both about what animals do.
   - Ⓓ They are both about how animals are named.

4. **From the stories, you can tell that jumbo became a new word**
   - Ⓐ after easel.
   - Ⓑ before easel.
   - Ⓒ in the 1600s.
   - Ⓓ at the same time as easel.

5. **The story "The Easel Guess" is made-up. It is not a true story, but it has true facts in it. What answer is a fact and not just part of the story?**
   - Ⓐ The word "easel" comes from the word "easy."
   - Ⓑ Ms. Ta explained that Jumbo was a real elephant.
   - Ⓒ The class thought an easel looked like a donkey.
   - Ⓓ Dutch painters called their standing frames 'ezels.'

Show What You Know (cont.)

6. Write down all the words you can think of that have the same meaning as jumbo.

_____   _____   _____

_____   _____   _____

7. Write down the two reasons Dutch painters called their standing frames 'ezels.'

1. _____

2. _____

Write two or more sentences that tell what each story is about.

8. "The Elephant that Made a Word" _____

_____

9. "The Easel Guess" _____

_____

10. Sometimes people will say, "Stop monkeying around!" What do people mean when they say this? Do you think an animal is behind this saying? Tell why or why not.

_____

_____

_____

Bibliography

"Achilles." *The New Encyclopedia Britannica*, volume 1, page 62. Encyclopedia Britannica, Inc., 1990.

Arlon, Penelope, Lorrie Mack, and Zahavit Shalev. *How People Live*. DK Publishing, Inc., 2003.

Aruego, Jose and Ariane Dewey. *Weird Friends: Unlikely Allies in the Animal Kingdom*. Gulliver Books, Harcourt, Inc., 2002.

Boyd, Shelley. "Bug Bowl Attracts Crowd with Cricket-Spitting Contest." *The Exponent*. April 19, 2004: A1.

Brust, Beth Wagner and Bob Dorn. *Zoobooks: Rattlesnakes*. Wildlife Education, Ltd., 1989.

Cohen, Sasha and Amanda Maciel. *Fire on Ice: Autobiography of a Champion Figure Skater*. HarperCollins Publishers, 2005.

Cordoba, Yasmine A. *Igloo*. The Rourke Book Company, Inc., 2001.

Crow, Joseph Medicine and Herman J. Viola. *Counting Crow: Becoming a Crow Chief on the Reservation and Beyond*. National Geographic Society, 2006.

Cunkle, Lorna. *Extreme Nature Knowledge Cards*. Pomegranate Communications, Inc., 2006.

Davis, Gibbs. *Wackiest White House Pets*. Scholastic Press, 2004.

Farran, Christopher. *Animals to the Rescue! True Stories of Animal Heroes*. Avon Books, HarperCollins Publishers, 2000.

Garvey, Kathy Keatly. "Fingered By a Bug." *UC Davis Magazine*. Fall 2007: 6.

Gray, Susan H. *The Skeletal System*. The Child's World, 2004.

Hansen, Rosanna. *Panda: A Guide Horse for Ann*. Boyds Mills Press, Inc., 2005.

Hayhurst, Chris. *Mountain Biking! Get on the Trail*. The Rosen Publishing Group, Inc., 2000.

Hempleman-Adams, David and Robert Uhlig. *Walking on Thin Ice: In Pursuit of the North Pole*. Orion Books, 1998.

Bibliography _(cont.)

Hendrickson, Robert. *QPB Encyclopedia of Word and Phrase Origins*. Facts on File, Inc., 1997.

Lace, William W. *Tiger Woods: Star Golfer*. Enslow Publishing, Inc., 1999.

McNair, Sylvia and Lynne Mansure. *Kenya*. Children's Press, Scholastic, Inc., 2001.

Moir, John. *Return of the Condor: The Race to Save Our Largest Bird from Extinction*. The Lyons Press, 2006.

Phillips, Louis. *Going Ape: Jokes From the Jungle*. Viking Kestrel, Penguin Books, Inc., 1988.

Powell, Corey S. "20 things You Didn't Know About Living in Space." *Discover*. November 2007: 88.

Rubel, David. *Mr. President: The Human Side of America's Chief Executives*. Time-Life Books, 1998.

Sullivan, Robert and Robert Andreas, Eds. *The Greatest Adventures of All Times*. Life Books, Time Inc., 2000.

Taylor, Bonnie Highsmith. *Women with Grit*. Perfection Learning, 2000.

Wexo, John Bonnett. *Zoobooks: Elephants*. Wildlife Education, Ltd., 1986.

Wechsler, Doug. *Rattlesnakes*. PowerKids Press, The Rosen Publishing Group, Inc., 2001.

Wulffson, Don L. *The Kid Who Invented the Trampoline: More Surprising Stories about Inventions*. Dutton Children's Books, 2001.

—. *Zoobooks: Seals and Sea Lions*. Wildlife Education, Ltd., 1992.

—. *Zoobooks: The Apes*. Wildlife Education, Ltd., 1991.

Internet

"Cricket Spitting." Wikipedia.
http://en.wikipedia.org/wiki/Cricket_spitting
accessed October 2, 2007

Answer Key

Unit 1
1. C
2. A
3. C
4. A
5. B
6. stop at curbs, go across busy streets, pick up keys, touch door handles, go into stores, go up stairs, get in cars and trains
7. what: taught to wait; where: cannot answer; when: never; why: to help someone who cannot see; how: with a clicker and food

Unit 2
1. A
2. C
3. B
4. B
5. D
6. South changes to North; Indian to Arctic; light to heavy; slept to died
7. It keeps your body heat close to you; keeps cold outside air away from you

Unit 3
1. B
2. B
3. D
4. A
5. C

6. Condors: tracked with radio tags, cools itself by going to bathroom on legs, one of the largest flying birds in world; Arctic terns: tracked with bands, migrates farther than any other bird; flies yearly from Arctic Circle to Antarctic Circle
7. 1—Shing walks on shore 3—Shing got ranger 5—ranger wrote down band number, date, and where bird found

Unit 4
1. B
2. D
3. B
4. D
5. A
6. butterflies: not found, proves car driven at night; insects: found, proves car was in California
7. 2,3,1,5,4

Unit 5
1. C
2. A
3. B
4. C
5. D
6. islands, homes, boats, rafts, fuel, tea, food

7. reeds: yes, no, yes, yes; bricks: no, yes, no, no

Unit 6
1. A
2. B
3. D
4. D
5. C
6. 4,2,5,1,3

Unit 7
1. B
2. D
3. C
4. A
5. D
6. fluids: water, orange juice, tea, apple juice
7. float: May 4 and June 20; drop: May 10 and 20, June 4 and 10

Unit 8
1. B
2. D
3. C
4. A
5. A
6. Day: eat fleas and bugs in burrow; Night: cling to mouse and eat fleas
7. 3,6,5,2,1,4

Unit 9
1. C
2. B
3. D
4. B
5. D

Answer Key (cont.)

6.

two wheels; one horse
7. Mr. Swan, Lori, Mr. Swan, Lori

Unit 10
1. C
2. A
3. D
4. C
5. B
6. Boy climbed stone wall; Binti Jua picked up boy; Binti Jua put down limp boy.
7. fact—largest apes, eat plants, have nose print

Unit 11
1. D
2. B
3. B
4. C
5. C
6. 1: water his horses; 2: bathe; 4: walk back home
7. Dear Ulla,; Your friend, Tamara

Unit 12
1. D
2. C
3. A
4. B
5. A

6.
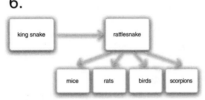
7. 9 segments

Unit 13
1. D
2. A
3. A
4. B
5. B
6. 1840: water; 1843: grass or horsehair; 1845: air
7. regular mountain, regular street, snow mountain

Unit 14
1. B
2. D
3. D
4. C
5. A
6. oldest tree: pine, over 4,725 years, California; longest snake: python, up to 33 feet (10 m), Asia
7. top row: Alejandro, Dana, Alejandro, Dana; middle row: mouse, dog, spider, dinosaur; bottom row: horse, bus, airplane, rocket ship

Unit 15
1. A
2. A
3. D

4. C
5. D
6. 4,2,1,5,3
7. B. and C.

Unit 16
1. C
2. D
3. D
4. C
5. A
6. sea lions: have ears, front flippers to push, rear flippers to steer; seals: no ears, front flippers to steer, rear flippers to push
7. what: to see a lion in the wild roar; where: cave on Oregon coast; when: Kate's birthday; why: to see wild sea lions; how: in an elevator

Unit 17
1. B
2. D
3. C
4. C
5. A
6. trim the lawn; eat the flowers
7. 1: Carol's mom; 2: lady walking dog; 3: boy at park; 5: Suzu's father

Unit 18
1. D
2. D
3. A

Answer Key (cont.)

4. C
5. A
6. legs—6; wings—4; antennas—2
7. 1: feathers, one corner; 2: straw, two corners; 3: candle and matches, entire room

Unit 19
1. C
2. B
3. A
4. C
5. B
6. before, after; after, before
7. possible answers: stained blue by snow, grew so fast could see grow, 42 ax handles could fit between eyes, took crow a day to fly between horns, could pull twisty roads straight, footprints became lakes

Unit 20
1. A
2. C
3. A
4. D
5. C
6. still learning: could check or not check turns in air, check slices boot toe, lands on two feet; knows the jump: check turns in air and lands on one foot

Unit 21
1. B
2. A
3. D
4. C
5. A
6. protects important organs in your body; holds you up; helps you move
7. Achilles is dipped in the waters of the River Styx; Achilles is killed by an arrow guided by Apollo.

Unit 22
1. D
2. D
3. C
4. A
5. C
6. what: homes for orphans; where: Kenya; when: mothers are shot; why: for their ivory tusks; how: keep switching around
7. 1: Kim was hunting elephants with a camera; 3: Kim took pictures of elephants bathing; or, Kim's guide told about elephant's trunks; 4: Kim sees elephants in mud and spraying dust, or, Kim's guide told how elephants protect themselves from insect bites.

Unit 23
1. A
2. B
3. B
4. C
5. D
6. noise: cough, jingle coins, rip open golf glove; movement: sit, turn, bend, wave
7. 1—Sanchez; 2—Tim; 3—Sanchez; 4—Tim; 5—Sanchez; 6—another teacher

Unit 24
1. A
2. A
3. B
4. C
5. B
6. ranch=station; girl ranch hand=jillaroo; boy ranch hand=jackaroo

Unit 25
1. B
2. B
3. A
4. A
5. D
6. large, big, huge, giant
7. 1—thought looked like a donkey; 2—carried a burden like a donkey